CUMBRIAN RAILWAYS

Sutton Publishing Limited
Phoenix Mill · Thrupp · Stroud
Gloucestershire · GL5 2BU

First published 1999

Title page: Ex-LMS Stanier 8F 2–8–0 No. 48708 with goods train on Shap Fell, 21 September 1962.

Half-title page: Straight through at Windermere station (*see* p. 21).

British Library Cataloguing in Publication Data
A catalogue record for this book is available from the British Library.

ISBN 0-7509-2043-2

Typeset in 10/11 Bembo.
Typesetting and origination by
Sutton Publishing Limited.
Printed in Great Britain by
Ebenezer Baylis, Worcester.

This book is dedicated to Preston Whiteley, rail enthusiast, who has so generously assisted with photographs and advice.

Carlisle station, August 1960. Sir William Stanier's second LMS 4–6–2 'Pacific' of 1933 (after *The Princess Royal* – 6200) 6201 (BR 46201) *Princess Elizabeth* is seen picking up passengers. This locomotive survived the end of steam scrapping.

CUMBRIAN RAILWAYS

JOHN MARSH & JOHN GARBUTT

SUTTON PUBLISHING LIMITED

The 0630 local stopping train from Hawick to Carlisle, ready to depart Hawick on the Waverley Line, Jun
1965. BR 4MT 2–6–0 No. 76049 is at the head (*see* p. 142).

CONTENTS

Introduction 7

1. London & North Western Railway 9

2. Midland Railway 37

3. North Eastern Railway 51

4. Furness Railway 59

5. Maryport & Carlisle Railway 91

6. Closed Lines Miscellany: 97

 The Little North Western – Kirkby Lonsdale to Lowgill 97

 'Kendal Tommy's' Line – Arnside to Hincaster Junction 101

 Lakeside Branch – Plumpton Junction to Lakeside and the Windermere Steamers 108

 Coniston Branch (Foxfield to Coniston) and the Coniston Steamers 117

 North Eastern – Tebay to Kirkby Stephen East Branch 122

 North Eastern – Penrith to Stainmore 128

 The CK&PR – Penrith to Workington 135

 The Waverley Line – Carlisle to the Border 142

 Brampton Junction to Alston 144

 Carlisle to Port Carlisle, Silloth and Solway Viaduct 146

 West Cumberland Lines 150

Index 160

Tebay sheds, 15 July 1960. Ex-LMS Fowler 4MT 2–6–4Ts of 1933, Nos 42396, 42404 and 42403 await banking duties.

INTRODUCTION

Before the arrival of the railways it is hard to imagine how difficult it was to travel through and from the ancient counties of Cumberland, Westmorland, Lancashire North of the Sands and the western tip of Yorkshire West Riding around Sedbergh and Dent. Each area had its peculiar problems. Those living near the coast could travel by sea; those in south Cumbria could travel, for a few years before the arrival of the railway, by 'express' barge on the Lancaster to Kendal canal! Otherwise travel was by horse-coach or on horseback, or on foot. Many of the routes went over steep hills so much climbing was required. Needless to say many people living in the area covered by the modern county of Cumbria never strayed very far from their own hearth. The arrival of the 'iron horse' changed everything.

The first railways to appear were those associated with industry where it was found that a wagon on a track could carry more, pulled by one horse, than a wagon on rough ground. In the north-east in particular the new mode of transport progressed with, of course, the cynics on the side saying, 'It can't last'. The first main railway line into the county of Cumberland came from the north-east and was opened in 1838. It ran from Newcastle to Carlisle, realizing a long desire by industrialists to link east with west. A decade later rail expansion was really under way with the north–south route completed in 1847. On the west coast the Furness Railway and the Maryport & Carlisle Railway were the largest of many local enterprises that opened lines in the mid-nineteenth century. The route through Keswick from Penrith to Workington was connected to the north-east by a railway down the Eden Valley and over Stainmore. Another connection to the north-east was made from the south via Kirkby Stephen, Tebay, Hincaster and Arnside. The glorious Settle–Carlisle was finished in 1876 when most of the other railway networks were already complete.

The wonderful scenery that brought tourists and the period of industrialization that produced new towns at Barrow-in-Furness and Millom and the conversion of many an old market town or seaport such as at Whitehaven, Workington, Maryport and Carlisle into a 'modern' working town meant that the population of the area rose rapidly and that it was a golden age for railways and all their services. The Furness Railway had lake steamers on two major lakes and ran a sea ferry business from Barrow. Railway company-sponsored hotels were built to cater for the new form of traveller. The expansion of tourism as a result of the arrival of the railways has probably left Cumbria with a larger legacy than the industry of those days, which has mostly been swept away and much of its ugly remains have been 'landscaped': a search for the iron and steel works at Ulverston, Barrow, Askam, Millom, Workington or other parts of the west coast reveals that there is little trace of them left now.

The run-down of the railways started in the Depression years of the 1930s and continued until very recently when it was suddenly realized that rails were an asset and not a liability. Roads had clogged with motor traffic and scientists pointed out that the exhaust emissions of all the motor vehicles were damaging the the environment. Railways offered possibilities that might help both problems. The Settle–Carlisle line was saved from what had seemed to be a fate of certain closure and there is talk of reopening many closed sections of railway not only for nostalgic but for sound commercial reasons. The old North British Railway's Waverley Line into Carlisle from Edinburgh would seem to be the most ambitious of the projects. Odd bits of Cumbrian track have never been closed; for instance, the Haverthwaite to Lakeside part of the old Furness Railway branch from Ulverston is now a holiday tourist attraction and at Alston a narrow gauge railway runs on the old trackbed. But in the main, closures, when they came, were extensive and nearly half this book is given over to coverage of the closed railways, the remains of which are to be found all over the county. The North Eastern Railway's lines seem to have suffered the most in terms of length of track closed, but along the west coast some of the small railway enterprises, absorbed in the great 1924 amalgamations, have disappeared altogether.

Both of the authors grew up when the London Midland & Scottish Railway had extensive lines in the Furness area. We watched the wartime use of the railways to and from Barrow and to various military storage areas, for instance the explosives and ammunition store at Plumpton quarry. The remaining iron and steel works in the area were in their last days but were working day and night and had a lot of rail traffic. A Webb 'Cauliflower' used to shunt coal wagons up to the Ulverston coal sheds after negotiating endless points between Plumpton and the ironworks and then travelling up the canal side.

Within the limitations of space we have attempted to give a multi-period train-spotter's view of Cumbrian railways – lots of locomotives, some famous, some not, and many, but not all, of the stations. The industrial traffic is shown. The tourist use of the railways is represented here too alongside the pleasure boats that waited at the end of train journeys. For good measure we have included humour from the early twentieth-century peak in rail travel: Cynicus and Valentine poked barbed wit at the branch lines. And for the first time in any book on Cumbrian railways we reveal that Alfred Aslett, Secretary of the Furness Railway, had a dog that collected postcards of 'dogs of all nations' – or so he apparently told his chairman the Duke of Devonshire! High-placed humour on the Furness Railway.

We hope we have not trodden on anyone's toes in the use of pictures and we have tried our best not to offend. We wish to acknowledge the help we have received from Mrs A. Bonnett of Allithwaite, Mr Peter Robinson of the Cumbrian Railways Association, Mr J. Fairer of Shap, Mr G. Dawson of Kendal, Mr D. Hinde of Brigham, Mr F. Holm of Kendal, Mr J. Matthews of Sedgwick, Mr F. Nevinson of Kendal, the Tourist Information Centre staff at Alston station, Mr N. Stead of Whitley Bay, and in particular Mr Preston Whiteley, a life-long rail enthusiast who allowed us free access to his wonderful photographic collection and offered his advice.

John Marsh and John Garbutt
Spring 1999

CHAPTER ONE

LONDON & NORTH WESTERN RAILWAY

Carlisle, May 1960 with ex-LMS Stanier 4–6–2 'Princess Coronation', BR No. 46238 City of Carlisle. *Note the Carlisle (Upperby) depot number 12B. The London & North Western Railway in Cumbria was developed because of the construction of a main line through the county* en route *from London to Glasgow. The west end of the Newcastle & Carlisle Railway had opened in 1836 and Carlisle was on the brink of becoming a railway town but the western main line from the south had only been built as far as mid-Lancashire. Then the Preston to Lancaster railway reached Lancaster in 1841. By 1843 it was possible to promote the Lancaster to Carlisle railway and, after many difficulties regarding the route and the increasing cost of labour, the rails reached Kendal in September 1846 (from where horse coaches took passengers further north). By mid-December of the same year the lines through to Carlisle were opened. Oxenholme, Tebay, Penrith and, of course, Carlisle were all junctions on the line and were set to become railway towns. By 1848 the route ran all the way to Glasgow as the Caledonian Railway carried the lines into Scotland, preceding the opening of the east coast railway to Edinburgh by two years. In 1846 the London & North Western Railway company was formed and gradually absorbed the Lancaster to Carlisle railway over the next thirteen years. In the decades that followed the LNWR took in other routes in Cumbria and gained ownership of the Lancaster to Kendal canal. The LNWR became part of the London, Midland & Scottish Railway in 1923/4.*

LNWR Webb 2–4–0 engine No. 5108 *Wyre* pulls a Carnforth to Oxenholme passenger train, *c.* 1910. Herman Prior's *Guide to the Lake District of England* (1890) says, 'At the important junction of Carnforth those who have up to this point travelled by the L&NW and whose destination is on the Furness line should be careful about changing carriages which in most cases is necessary. If on the other hand you proceed direct north to Oxenholme Junction you must also look out for a change of train.'

Burton & Holme station, *c.* 1905. The first station in Cumbria for LNWR trains travelling north, Burton & Holme (it was situated halfway between the two villages) also had a goods yard linked to nearby mills and was used by a local limestone quarry. The passenger station was an early British Railways' closure in 1950.

Milnthorpe station. The view above is from the beginning of the twentieth century looking south from the road bridge, while below the view is reversed in 1963 as the afternoon Windermere to Liverpool train travels south under the road bridge hauled by ex-LMS Fowler 4MT 2–6–4T No. 42319. The goods sidings at Milnthorpe brought much business to the railway, as a gunpowder works at Gatebeck had a 3½-mile private horse-drawn tramway connection which terminated at Milnthorpe station and the nearby dairy produce factory took goods both in and out via the railway.

Oxenholme engine sheds, 1962/3. This was an early site for a shed for banking engines even before the adjoining Kendal Junction (now Oxenholme) station was built. The 1970s' electrification of the main line finally saw the end of this facility. The top picture shows the scene from the south in 1963, and below on 2 December 1962 ex-LMS Fowler 2–6–4T No. 42322, showing shed plate 12C (Carlisle Canal), can be seen. Its front lamp shows branch freight duties (*see also* p. 16).

Oxenholme, *c.* 1900. LNWR 'Waterloo' class 1P 2–4–0 No. 829 is seen with a train of twelve passenger coaches approaching Oxenholme off the Windermere branch. This engine did not, unlike engines in its class on pages 10 and 23, survive until the LMS amalgamation in 1923.

Oxenholme, July 1963. A complete contrast with the picture above is this BR 4–6–2, No. 70053 on the 'Lakes Express' near the water point at the end of the main line Down platform on 26 July 1963. The words 'Waiting to leave for Penrith with the Keswick portion' are written on the back of the photograph. This 'Britannia' class locomotive was the next to last in its class and carried the name *Moray Firth*. Its first shed was Glasgow. The 'Lakes Express' deposited coaches at Lancaster (for the Furness line), Oxenholme (for Windermere) and then ran through Penrith to Keswick.

Oxenholme, October 1962. Type 4 English Electric Diesel No. D293 is seen on the Up line with a Dow
train at Oxenholme on 7 October. These locomotives were introduced from the late 1950s and caused muc
interest among both passengers and train-spotters. The shorter platforms than those of today can clearly b
seen along with the pedestrian crossing and the Down platform water-point. All have now gone.

)xenholme, 24 March 1962. 'Britannia' class 4–6–2 No. 70026 *Polar Star* on the Up platform. These 94-ton ıonsters had only six more years to run as steam was abandoned in 1968. Train-spotting would never be the ıme again. At that time passenger traffic levels were falling and there was much debate about the future of ıilways. Oxenholme did not suffer as much as nearby Tebay (*see* pp. 25–6 and 122–4) as the branch line to Vindermere remained open. The goods yard, engine sheds and depot have all gone but passenger traffic ırough the station is now at a very healthy level even if the branch train does not wait for a late main line :ain anymore.

A glimpse of Oxenholme in 1905 is seen in the Bulmer's *Guide* of that year. Under Natland parish are listed: 'homas Collins, Locomotive foreman, Hill Place; William Conway, Platelayer, 3 Helmside; R. Koster, Lefreshment Room, Oxenholme Station; Benjamin T. Porter, Signalman, Holme Lane; Henry Preston, tationmaster, Oxenholme Station; James Tideswell, Permanent Way Inspector, Natland Terrace; Wigan Coal & 'on Company, Oxenholme Goods Station, C.E. Greenall, agent, Edw. Bateson, manager.

)*pposite*: Oxenholme, September 1961. BR 9F 2–10–0 freight engine No. 92072 passes the main line Down latform water-point and platform signal on 2 September (*see also* p. 42 for this class of engine). The layout of)xenholme station was to be altered as electrification approached in the 1970s.

Kendal station, 1963. Fowler 4MT class 2–6–4T No. 42322 (*see also* p. 12) is seen at Kendal station on the 4.55 p.m. Windermere to Oxenholme train. The canopies on both the Up and Down platforms can be clearly seen. The main station building is now a doctors' surgery and chemist's shop and the platforms have been changed into the 'unmanned halt' style.

Burneside station, *c.* 1902. The six-coach train is pulled by a LNWR tank engine. The opening of this branch line in 1847 came only two years after James Cropper acquired the paper mill nearby. It was not long before a small private railway linked the paper mills with the branch line and enhanced the prosperity of both enterprises.

Staveley station. The picture above is from about 1905 with Stationmaster William Parrington standing on the Up platform with his staff. Below, the afternoon Crewe to Windermere train comes into the Down platform on 18 August 1962 hauled by ex-LMS Stanier 5MT 4–6–0 No. 44709. Prior's *Guide* of 1890 told travellers, 'From Kendal the line runs up the Kent Valley to Staveley where all tickets are collected.' Since 1971 Staveley has been an unmanned halt.

'To Windermere and back in one day.' Branch line humour – Cynicus did not omit the Windermere branch from his barbed comments on branch line speed. These postcards from the first decade of the twentieth century sold well at busy resorts such as Windermere.

On the Windermere Branch, 18 August 1962. The afternoon Windermere to Liverpool train is seen here hauled by ex-LMS Stanier 'Jubilee' class 6P 4–6–0 No. 45627 *Sierra Leone*. The branch was made into a single track elongated siding in 1973.

Windermere station, *c.* 1900. Prior's 1890 *Guide* states, 'There is a liberal provision of conveyances of all kinds: Coaches for Ambleside, Rydal, Grasmere and Keswick; Omnibuses for Bowness and Low Wood and any number of other vehicles to reach more secluded haunts.' The station building is now a supermarket and the lamp-cum-drinking fountain is in the garden of Kendal's Brewery Arts centre.

Windermere station yard, *c.* 1910. An early motor charabanc with a large radiator (which was an attempt to stop overheating in the hilly area) has posed for the photographer. A Riggs' horse-coach driver in white top hat sits in the back. It would have been hard to imagine then the later demise of both the railway and the horse-coaches as the motor bus took over.

Fares to Windermere Village

FROM VARIOUS TOWNS.

The ordinary tourist fares are given first, and the cheap week-end fares below in italic.

Birmingham	45/3	—	23/-
	26/-	—	*13/-*
Bristol	68/-	—	34/-
	41/-	—	*20/6*
Glasgow	49/9	—	24/-
Liverpool	33/3	—	12/-
	16/-	—	*8/-*
London	73/4	42/-	38/-
	39/-	*30/6*	*22/6*
Manchester	23/9	—	12/-
	16/-	—	*8/-*
Newcastle	28/10	—	15/-
	15/3	—	*8/6*
Cheap Fares for 10 days...	*22/-*	—	*11/9*

Fares to Keswick

FROM VARIOUS TOWNS.

Birmingham	55/-	—	28/-
	32/-	—	*16/-*
Bristol	80/4	—	41/-
Glasgow	39/6	—	20/3
London	81/-	47/6	33/-
	44/-	*34/6*	*25/3*
Newcastle	26/8	—	14/-

Fares to Penrith

FROM VARIOUS TOWNS.

Birmingham	50/6	—	25/-
Bristol	75/10	—	37/-
Glasgow	39/6	—	20/3
London	76/6	—	40/-
Newcastle	22/2	—	11/-

Fares to Windermere, 1900. Pearson's *Gossipy Guide to the English Lakes* included all the information that a traveller would need to get to the Lake District including fares to Windermere, Keswick and Penrith. A London & North Western Railway guide of the same period says, 'Windermere and Keswick lie but a very short distance away from the main line of the West Coast Royal Mail route, which is celebrated for the excellence of its permanent way and its rolling stock and passengers travelling by this line are sure of every modern and up-to-date convenience as well as of civility, attention and punctuality. Some of the trains afford the convenience of taking luncheon or dinner in specially fitted up cars *en route* and with all the trains luncheon baskets, hot or cold, can readily be obtained at the principal stations. Windermere station in the village of Windermere is at a distance of one and a half miles from the lake at Bowness. Four in hand coaches run between Windermere station and Keswick calling at Ambleside and Grasmere.'

ccident at Windermere, 1962. The train from Blackpool had arrived at Windermere station at 12.22 p.m. and ne three carriages were being shunted on to platform 2 to make up the 6.56 train from Windermere. The sual system was for an engine to pull the carriages to a point where they could be released and gravity-witched into another platform. On 13 August 1962 the brakesman, Thomas Batley, realizing that the brakes on wo of the carriages had failed, jumped clear as the coaches entered the station 'at great speed' according to the *Vestmorland Gazette* of the following Friday – 'Miracle no one was hurt' was the headline. In all 50 ft of station eranda was demolished together with five pillars supporting the brick and stone forecourt awning. Only a ew minutes earlier the yard adjoining 'had been thronged with people' and a youth with a cycle who had een seen there for some time was suspected to have been lost underneath the carriage. He could not be raced and no one was injured in the incident. With some difficulty the two runaway coaches, the front one aving lost a set of bogie wheels, were pulled back into the station (*see also* p. 3).

North from Oxenholme. London & North Western Bowen-Cooke class 3P 4–6–2T No. 1184 (LMS No. 6976) northbound leaving Oxenholme towards Grayrigg, probably about the time of the First World War. This class of engine was scrapped by the LMS in the late 1930s and early 1940s.

Banking at Grayrigg in the late nineteenth century. Two Webb 2–4–0 engines can be seen at Grayrigg box. A mixed passenger/goods train is being hauled north up the bank while the other waits by the signal box to assist. A close-up of one of this class of engine can be seen opposite.

Grayrigg station, *c.* 1900. Staff and passengers are waiting for the next train on the London & North Western Railway. Grayrigg station was closed to passengers in 1954 and, after much advertising by the British Railways Board for someone to buy the buildings, the site was cleared.

A Webb engine, *c.* 1900. This example of the 2–4–0 engines from the 1890s was No. 764; it was given the name *Shap* and thus became a 'local' engine. The LMS withdrew the last of the class in the 1930s although one of them, No. 790 *Hardwicke*, was preserved and is now at the National Railway Museum in York.

Dillicar troughs. Above, two northbound LNWR express engines with a train on Dillicar troughs between Grayrigg and Tebay before 1920. The leading engine is Whale 3P 4–6–0 No. 2643 *Bacchus,* which would get the number 5530 from the LMSR, and following is Whale 2P 4–4–0 No. 561 *Antaeus*, which became No. 5245. Below, in BR days ex-LMS 'Black Five' Stanier 5MT class 4–6–0 No. 45191 picks up water as it heads north with a long goods train. Train-spotters at the Dillicar troughs were always sure of a fine sight.

ɔay station. In the picture above the station is seen from the south in the 1930s. Tebay was also a railway ɔot with extensive sidings and was the junction between the south and the north-east. The passenger station s the centre of the village which grew up round the railway and it included a WH Smith bookstall and a ·eshments room. Passengers could leave the main line here for stations to and beyond Kirkby Stephen. .ow, the train in the platform is an enthusiasts' 'special' in 1960 pulled by ex-1886 North Eastern Railway ɔrsdell J21 class 0–6–0 No. 65033, which was having a second lease of life at the time before being finally :hdrawn in 1962 (*see also* p. 53).

Tebay. In the picture above a Manchester to Glasgow express is taken north on 4 August 1954 from the t busy Tebay station by 'Royal Scot' class 4–6–0 express locomotive No. 46121 *Highland Light Infantry – The* (*of Glasgow Regiment*. The extensive sidings and sheds can be seen surrounding the station, which was origin shared by the London & North Western Railway and the North Eastern Railway. *Opposite*, another of once famous class of engines, which were first introduced in 1927, is seen in February 1960 at Scout Gr signal box just north of Tebay on the main line. This was No. 46165 *The Ranger – 12th London Regt*. Sce such as these drew railway enthusiasts to the Tebay/Shap area for many decades. Closure of Tebay facilities t place between 1952 and 1968 and now the only remains of this once busy junction is the main l north–south. Many houses in Tebay village stood empty for years after the closures as families sought w elsewhere (*see also* p. 122).

46165

'Aberdeen Express' on Shap Summit, pre-1904. An LNWR Webb 2–4–0 pulls a nine-coach express train north over Shap Fell. This picture appeared in the 1904 series of postcards issued by the LNWR. Shap Summit is the highest point on the London to Carlisle route at 916 ft and the provision of extra banking engines to get many trains up the notorious 1:75 gradient must have cost many thousands of pounds.

Shap Fells, September 1960. 'Black Five' 4–6–0 No. 44942 double-heads an approximately twelve-coach express train pulled by an unknown 4–6–2 over Shap. The pulling power of these combined engines made light work of the notorious gradient.

Empties for Shap Quarry, 22 August 1959. Ivatt 'Mogul' class 4 No. 43028 heads empty ballast wagons up the gradient to Shap Quarry (just off the Summit). The Shap Quarry produced two sorts of granite and had a large siding which, at one time, climbed the fell to the adjoining 'pink rock' quarry. Its proximity to the main line has ensured continuing business for the railway from the time of the LNWR right through to today.

Shap station, *c.* 1905. An unknown LNWR locomotive pulls a three-coach, probably local, train into Shap station. It is interesting to note the goods siding and platform signal-box, gone since the 1960s' closures. The LNWR guide contemporary with this photograph says, 'Shap is the station for the beautiful little Haweswater, five-and-a-half miles away.'

Clifton Moor station, 1940s. The main line to the north from Shap came to Clifton and Lowther station much used by Lord Lonsdale from nearby Lowther Castle until its closure in 1938. Clifton Moor was the first station on the North Eastern line after its junction with the LNWR but was not opened until 1927. For about ten years Clifton village had two passenger stations. The closure of the North Eastern line was a slow process: the through route from Penrith to Darlington was shut down in 1962 leaving only a quarry line to Merry Gill, Kirkby Stephen. This closed in the 1970s leaving the branch through Clifton to Warcop camp for military use until this too closed in recent times (*see* p. 128 for more on the Eden Valley line).

Penrith station. Crowded motor charabancs and horse coaches pick up passengers at about the time of the First World War. The London & North Western Railway guide of a decade or so earlier had said, 'Penrith, eleven and a half miles from Shap, is best known as the departure point for Keswick and Ullswater and can be considered the northern gateway to the Lake District.' Between Penrith and Carlisle there were small stations at Plumpton, Calthwaite, Southwaite and Wreay.

NDON and NORTH WESTERN RAILWAY.

HALF-DAY, ONE DAY, and WEEK-END FARES.

To PENRITH.

STATIONS.	Days upon which One Day Tickets are issued.	Days upon which Half-Day Tickets are issued.	Third Class. Half-Day.	One Day.	Week-end.
			s. d.	s. d.	s. d.
Carlisle	Thurs. and Sats.	Thurs. and Sats.	1 3	1 9	2 0
Calthwaite	..	Do.	0 9	..	..
Carnforth	Mons., Thurs. & Sats.	..	..	3 3	4 0
Ingleton	Do.	..	..	3 6	4 3
Kendal	Do.	..	..	2 9	3 6
Kirkby Lonsdale	Do.	..	..	3 0	3 9
Lancaster	Mons., Weds. & Sats.	..	..	3 6	4 3
Milnthorpe	Mons., Thurs. & Sats.	..	..	3 3	4 0
Morecambe	Mons., Weds. & Sats.	..	..	3 6	4 3
Bare Lane	Do.	..	..	3 6	4 3
Plumpton	..	Thurs. and Sats.	0 6	..	..
Preston	Mons., Thurs. & Sats.	..	..	4 0	6 6
Sedbergh	Do.	..	..	2 9	3 0
Southwaite	..	Thurs. and Sats.	1 0	..	..
Staveley	Do.	..	..	3 0	3 9
Windermere	Mons., Thurs & Sats.	..	..	3 3	4 0
Wreay	..	Do.	1 0	..	..

Half-Day and One Day tickets are available on day of issue only, by certain specified trains. For particulars of availability see Railway Company's Bills.

WEEK-END TICKETS are issued on Fridays and Saturdays by ANY Train having a through connection, and are available for return on following Sunday, Monday, or Tuesday, by ANY Train having a through connection (Corridor Trains excepted in both directions).

WEEKLY EXCURSIONS are also run from London (Euston) to Penrith every Thursday during the Season (June to September, Bank Holidays excepted), returning on the following Monday, Thursday, Monday week, or Thursday week, at the following Fare :—25s. For further particulars with reference to outward and return times, etc., apply Supt. of the Line, Euston Station.

Cheap tickets to Penrith, 1903. The Ullswater Steam Navigation Company had a large section on train services in its early guides. Details could be obtained from the various companies including: North Eastern, Midland, Lancashire & Yorkshire, Great Northern, Great Eastern, Great Western, Great Central, Caledonian, Furness and Glasgow & South Western in addition to the LNWR (*see also* p. 46).

The bookstall at Carlisle station, *c.* 1900. The John Menzies bookstall at Carlisle at the turn of the century was in the centre of a busy station built about half a century before by the Lancaster & Carlisle Railway and the Caledonian Railway. At the end of the nineteenth century seven railway companies shared the facilities.

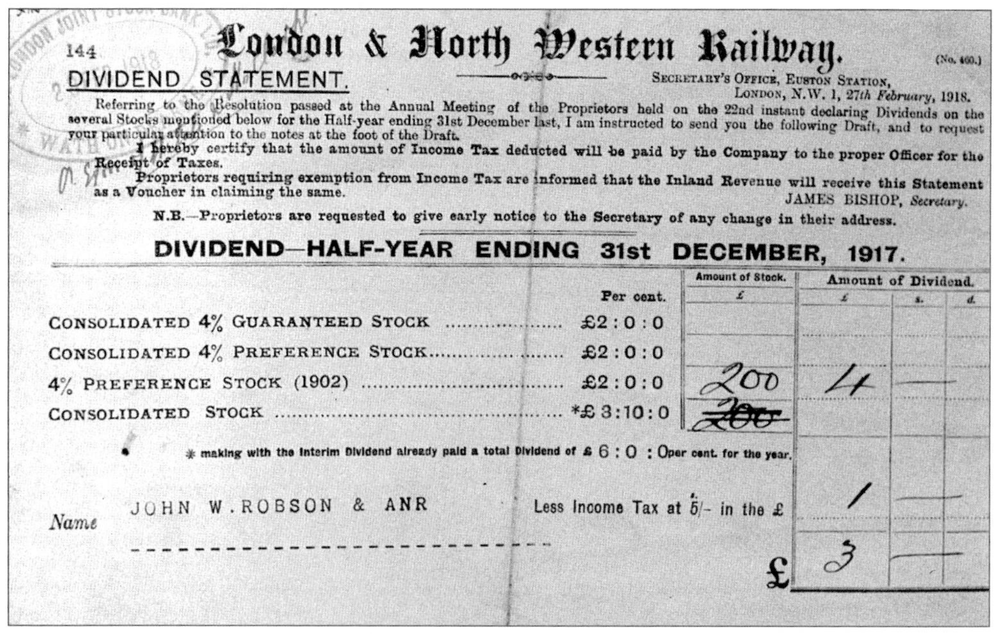

144 **London & North Western Railway.** (No. 460.)

DIVIDEND STATEMENT.

SECRETARY'S OFFICE, EUSTON STATION,
LONDON, N.W. 1, *27th February*, 1918.

Referring to the Resolution passed at the Annual Meeting of the Proprietors held on the 22nd instant declaring Dividends on the several Stocks mentioned below for the Half-year ending 31st December last, I am instructed to send you the following Draft, and to request your particular attention to the notes at the foot of the Draft.

I hereby certify that the amount of Income Tax deducted will be paid by the Company to the proper Officer for the Receipt of Taxes.

Proprietors requiring exemption from Income Tax are informed that the Inland Revenue will receive this Statement as a Voucher in claiming the same.

JAMES BISHOP, *Secretary.*

N.B.—Proprietors are requested to give early notice to the Secretary of any change in their address.

DIVIDEND—HALF-YEAR ENDING 31st DECEMBER, 1917.

	Per cent.	Amount of Stock. £	Amount of Dividend. £	s.	d.
CONSOLIDATED 4% GUARANTEED STOCK	£2 : 0 : 0				
CONSOLIDATED 4% PREFERENCE STOCK	£2 : 0 : 0				
4% PREFERENCE STOCK (1902)	£2 : 0 : 0	200	4	—	
CONSOLIDATED STOCK	*£ 3 : 10 : 0	~~200~~			
* making with the Interim Dividend already paid a total Dividend of £ 6 : 0 : 0 per cent. for the year.					
Name JOHN W. ROBSON & ANR — Less Income Tax at 5/- in the £			1	—	
		£	3	—	

LNWR Dividend Certificate, 1917. Like the Furness Railway (*see* p. 79) the LNWR did well during the First World War, paying 4 per cent on most stock, but unfortunately for the shareholders income tax had climbed to 25 per cent.

ırlisle station, 27 August 1960. Ex-LMS 'Jubilee' class 4–6–0 express passenger locomotive *Sans pareil*, ırrying its BR number 45732 and the Carlisle Kingmoor depot number 12A, stands at Carlisle waiting for e 'go' signal. (*See* p. 86 for another engine with the same name; the title was originally given to a very early comotive on the Manchester to Liverpool line.) The lamp configuration shows express passenger duties. ıis class of engine was designed by Sir William Stanier of the LMS in 1934 and was first brought into rvice in 1935, the twenty-fifth year in the reign of George V. The first engine in the class carried the name *lver Jubilee*.

Carlisle station, 1890s. The Caledonian Railway was involved from the start with the Lancaster & Carlisl Railway in the building of Citadel station at Carlisle. Above, Caledonian 4–4–0 engine No. 66 is seen a Carlisle in the late nineteenth century. A few of this type of locomotive survived through to BR days. Th Caledonian Railway ran through Carlisle to stations on its own lines in north Cumberland. Below, tw LNWR Webb 2–4–0 engines head a turn-of-the-century 'Scotch Express'.

arlisle, 12 August 1960. British Railways 'Clan' class 6P 4–6–2 No. 72001 (the second in its class) *Clan ameron* sits at Carlisle station on an Up 'Scottish Express'. *Clan Buchanan* was the first in the class (No. 72000) hich was introduced in 1952. Only eight years old when the photograph was taken, these amazing express eam engines had less than eight years left to run as the age of steam came to an end and train-spotting lost uch of its excitement. By 1960 diesel engines had already started to appear on main line expresses but the ectrification scheme was some years away from the north-west main line. Carlisle was at this time the nction with the Waverley Line that ran to Edinburgh and it is likely that this express had used that route (*see o* p. 142, 'Closed Lines').

John of Gaunt in trouble at Carlisle. Its title seems to be from the fourteenth century and more relevant to the Lancaster end of the line but – as these pictures taken at Kingmoor, Carlisle show – British Railways' 'Britannia' class 4–6–2 No. 70012 *John of Gaunt* was indeed in trouble on 17 September 1966 after a collision at Kingmoor. The end of steam in 1968 was near and scrapping must have been considered, but the engine was repaired at Crewe and was put back in service to be later photographed by Peter Robinson of the Cumbrian Railways Association on a football special at Carlisle in January 1967. It was, says Peter, one of a dozen 'Britannia' locomotives withdrawn from Carlisle when Kingmoor sheds closed in 1967.

CHAPTER TWO

MIDLAND RAILWAY

Kirkby Stephen West, 11 June 1960. Ex-LMS heavy freight locomotive Stanier 8F 2–8–0 No. 48676 heads south on the old Midland Railway Settle–Carlisle line. The Midland Railway built the Settle–Carlisle line between 1869 and 1875 and it has been described as 'the last great work executed in Britain by navvies working in the traditional way.' Arguments between the London & North Western Railway and the Midland Railway over running on the 'Little North Western' route (see p. 97) caused the Midland line to apply for parliamentary permission to use a different route but after permission was granted and the route costed and surveyed the Midland Railway thought it was not such a good idea after all. The company was, however, forced to go ahead and as a result the country was given some of the finest railway engineering ever carried out. The line enters Cumbria from the south at the top of the Pennine ridge. Prior to local government reorganization in 1974 Westmorland was not reached until the top of Mallerstang, but now the trains – having crossed the famous Ribblehead viaduct and been through the infamous 2,629 yards of the Blea Moor tunnel – pop into Cumbria at Dent Head with its magnificent Dent Head and Arten Gill viaducts. The line then runs through Cumbria to Carlisle. Close to closure in recent years, the line now seems to have an assured future as more and more business is put back onto its rails.

Dent Head, 16 July 1960. Ex-LMS 'Black Five' class 5MT 4–6–0 No. 44790 runs south over the Dent Head viaduct towards Blea Moor tunnel. The line in Dentdale north from this point is on a terrace on the valley side until it reaches Dent station.

Dent station, *c.* 1905. The station opened in 1867 and was proclaimed to be the highest on a main line in England at 1,150 ft above sea level. It is some 4 miles and 400 ft up from the village from which it takes its name. The station should possibly have been called Monkey Beck or Coal Road but obviously the misleading Dent sounded better. It is now an unmanned halt, reopened after some years of complete closure.

Aisgill, 1960. A busy scene of tracklaying at Aisgill at the top of the Mallerstang valley in 1960 shows complete new sections of track being put in place. An English Electric diesel-electric 0–6–0 shunter was being used on the work train of crane wagon and workmen's coach. The weather looks to be the usual rain associated with the Pennines in north Westmorland.

The Aisgill train disaster, 24 December 1910. 'Scotch Express wrecked – appalling disaster near Kirkby Stephen' ran the headline in the *Mid Cumberland and North Westmorland Herald* of 31 December 1910. 'The scene of the catastrophe,' continued the report, 'was Aisgill, a lonely and exposed moorland just north of Hawes Junction. It is the summit level whence the Midland line descends into the Eden Valley and the highest section of main line in England. The Midland Express, which left St Pancras at midnight on Friday for Carlisle and Glasgow, collided at Aisgill about 6 a.m. on Saturday with two pilot engines which had been assisting heavier trains southwards and were returning to Carlisle at about 25 miles an hour. The Express, drawn by two engines, which had been travelling at 60 miles an hour, dashed into them with disastrous results. The pilot engines were derailed and carried a distance of about 150 yards along the line while both the Express locomotives jumped the metals and dashed into the bank on the left-hand side of the track. . . . The terrible confusion was made all the worse by the fact that the restaurant cars subsequently caught fire. . . . Twelve persons, one of them a child, were trapped in the first two carriages, which were telescoped by the impact with the leading goods van and all twelve were either killed outright or burned to death. Several other passengers were cut and bruised.' The report continues with many details of the accident as given by witnesses at the scene as the train burned, and the evidence of Dr Ernest Hugh Kitchen of Skipton at the following Monday's inquest. Dr Kitchen had difficulty in saying how many bodies there were in the parts of the train he examined. The whole gory report was made more poignant because all had been travelling to Scotland for Christmas. This photograph shows the scene at the worst part of the disaster on the day of the crash with workmen and officials by the still smoking wreckage.

Opposite: Aisgill, 28 August 1960. LMS-built and Midland Railway-designed Fowler 4F 0–6–0 class goods locomotive No. 44467 pulls its train up Aisgill, above, while below a similar locomotive, No. 43993, is pictured near the same location on similar duties on the same day. This once extensive class of goods engine (over 700 were built) were of course at home on the ex-Midland Railway's Settle–Carlisle line.

44467

Near Birkett tunnel, Kirkby Stephen, August 1960. A goods train leaves Birkett tunnel pulled by a Hughes–Fowler 6P/5F class 2–6–0 engine No. 42833. The workers constructing Birkett tunnel during the 1870s found they were digging through the Pennine fault with shale, limestone, grit, slate, iron, coal and lead all to be found in its 424-yard length.

Kirkby Stephen West, June 1960. British Rail 9F class heavy goods 2–10–0 locomotive No. 92015 pulls a goods train out of the siding at Kirkby Stephen West station. These very efficient engines made light work of the Settle–Carlisle but had a short life because they were built as the decision to scrap steam was in the making. The last of 251 engines was named *Evening Star* and ran for five years only from 1960.

Smardale Gill viaduct, 1930s. LMS 4–6–2 No. 6200 *The Princess Royal* pulls the 'Thames–Forth Express' (later renamed 'The Waverley') south over the Smardale Gill viaduct, which at 130 ft is one of the highest on the line. This engine, built in 1933, gave its name to a class of Stanier-designed engines in the 8P class of LMS express passenger locomotives (*see also* pp. 4 and 9).

Leaving Crosby Garrett tunnel, 11 July 1959. Ex-LMS Stanier 8F 2–8–0 No. 48464 leaves Crosby Garrett tunnel with a sheeted set of wagons. Over 800 of this type of locomotive were built after 1935. Crosby Garrett station (*see* p. 44) approach from the south included the Smardale Gill viaduct, the tunnel, a 55 ft-high viaduct built over the village and then the 55 ft-deep cutting in which the station was built.

Crosby Garrett station, April 1962. A 1920s LMS Hughes–Fowler 2–6–0, No. 42771, pulls a lengthy goods train through the ruins of Crosby Garrett station. The platforms had gone and the buildings were falling into ruin following the pre-Beeching closures of the 1950s. The station had been opened on 1 May 1876 when railways allowed the inhabitants of this ancient village and surrounding hamlets easy access to the rest of the country. Families who had resided in these remote parts for centuries and hardly left the area found themselves easily able to visit market towns and holiday resorts that their parents could have but dreamed of visiting. Kelly's 1897 directory advised readers, 'Crosby Garrett is on the Midland Railway, Stationmaster David Reynolds. The telegraph office is at the station. It is 1 mile from Smardale station on the North Eastern Railway.' The small remote population obviously did not fit into postwar railway economics and now their nearest stations are at Kirkby Stephen on the old Midland route and Penrith and Oxenholme on the old LNWR.

Appleby station, 20 April 1949. Stanier class 5MT 4–6–0 No. 45017 takes a goods train through. Prior's *Guide* of 1890 said, 'Appleby is a notable example of decadence. Once a town of probably 20,000 inhabitants it is now very small and unimportant with perhaps 5,000 persons in the urban district. Perhaps the old town may again flourish for of late years two important railways (the Midland and the North Eastern) have been extended thereto thus bringing the formerly out-of-the-way place into easier rapid communication with any part of the kingdom.' (*See also* p. 129.)

Longmarton station in the 1920s. The station after Appleby on the line towards Carlisle was Longmarton built in the typical Midland railway architectural style. Other stations were at Newbiggin, Culgaith, Langwathby, Salkeld, Lazonby, Armathwaite, Cotehill, Cumwhinton and Scotby. Longmarton station opened in 1876 and was closed in 1968.

MIDLAND RAILWAY.

Grand Day Trips to Lake Ullswater.

EVERY DAY, during July, August and September
(except August 1st and 3rd, and Sundays),

To Parties of 10 or more, Cook's Cheap Day Excursion Tickets to

PATTERDALE

INCLUDING RAILWAY, CONVEYANCES, AND STEAMER,
Will be issued.

Times of starting and Fare there and back :—

FROM		a.m.	Additional train up to Sept. 12th.	INCLUSIVE FARE. To return same day only. Third Class Railway and Second Class on Steamer.*
			a.m.	
Leeds (Wellington), by train	dep.	6 0	6 40	7/9
Bradford (Midland station), by train ..	,,	6 10	6 40	
Langwathby, by Coach or Conveyance	,,	10 0	10 0	
		p.m.	p.m.	
Pooley Bridge, on Ullswater Lake, by steamer	,,	12 15	12 15	
Patterdale, by steamer	arr.	1 0	1 0	

* *On payment of 6d. extra passengers can travel first class on the steamer.*

☛ The trains will call at Leeds, Bradford, Manningham, Frizinghall, Shipley, Keighley, Skipton, &c., both going and returning, for passengers by this excursion, but tickets will not be issued at the Railway Stations, and they can only be obtained in advance at Messrs. Cook & Son's excursion offices at Leeds and Bradford, as below.

The return steamer leaves PATTERDALE at 3.55 p.m., conveyances leave POOLEY BRIDGE at 4.40 p.m., passing Yanwath, King Arthur's Round Table, Brougham Hall, Edenhall, &c., &c., and return train leaves LANGWATHBY (Midland Railway) at 8.47 p.m. the same day.

Passengers are requested to verify times in case of alteration.

Arrangements can be made with Messrs. Cook & Son for Meals or Refreshments either at Penrith, Pooley Bridge, or Patterdale; particulars furnished on application.

Near Cotehill, *c.* 1937. An LMSR eight-coach double-headed express is seen on the Midland line near Cotehill. The 4–4–0 Midland-designed but LMS-built (in 1925) Johnson 'Compound' No. 1148 leads LMS Stanier 'Jubilee' class 4–6–0 No. 5652 *Hawke*. Both were given an extra number 4 at the beginning of their original number when British Railways took over the LMS.

Opposite: Advertising Midland Railway trips to Ullswater. The post-First World War guide issued by the Ullswater Steam Navigation Company included advertising by the Midland and other railway companies (*see also* p. 31). The Midland Railway also offered a 'Day Outings' programme which gave details of day trips for parties of ten or more at greatly reduced prices. Langwathby station was used as a change-over point from rail to coach for the Ullswater trips. Other trip destinations included Penrith where Appleby station was used and where passengers were advised to 'find their own way between one station and the other' (not too difficult as they are virtually next door to each other).

Armathwaite, 1920s. A famous picture of a famous engine – Johnson Compound class 4P 4–4–0 takes a 'Scotch Express' through Armathwaite after the LMS took over the Midland Railway but with MR still displayed on the buffer beam. This engine had a different number until the MR allocated 1000 in 1907. Built in 1902, it was altered many times in its long working life up to 1952 when it was rebuilt again to run special trains for ten more years. It is now part of the National Collection at York.

Carlisle, *c.* 1924. A southbound express on the Midland line pulls out of Carlisle at about the time of the formation of the LMSR. The engines double-heading the train are Johnson Compound design 2P class 4–4–0 No. 412 (in front) and Johnson–Deeley Compound 4P class 4–4–0 No. 1071 (built in 1924). The words 'The 12.10 ex Carlisle' are written on the back of the card.

Carlisle, 1959. A class of locomotive designed and built by the Midland Railway from 1911 was to be popular with the LMSR from 1924 – it is reported to have built 575 of them. The Midland Fowler 4F 0–6–0 was a maid of all work and can be seen on pp. 41, 90 and 150. Here number 44009 (built by the Midland Railway) is seen in British Railways days at work at Carlisle station.

Kingmoor Depot, Carlisle, 17 September 1966. An ex-Midland Railway designed locomotive much used through to British Railways days was the 0–6–0 tank engine. Here two are seen in steam at Kingmoor as Preston Whiteley recorded the last years of steam at Carlisle. Fowler 0–6–0T No. 47471 stands in front of its unrecorded companion.

'Scotch Express' approaching Carlisle. A Midland Railway Deeley 4P 4–4–0 No. 997 is seen bringing the Midland Railway express into Carlisle at about the time of the First World War. The engine was the last of a class based on the famous Johnson design; all were withdrawn from service in early LMS days.

Platform 3 at Carlisle station, *c.* 1910. A party of officials greets the Midland Railway express on the retirement of a senior member of Citadel station's staff. A Johnson Midland Railway 1P 2–4–0 No. 181 leads what appears to be a 4–4–0 Compound.

CHAPTER THREE

NORTH EASTERN RAILWAY

Carlisle, 27 August 1960. 4–6–2 No. 60100 Spearmint *was an ex-London & North Eastern Railway A3 'Pacific' of the class designed by Sir Nigel Gresley in 1922, his last year with the Great Northern Railway before it became part of the LNER. The North Eastern Railway took over the Newcastle & Carlisle Railway – which had brought the first main line into Carlisle between 1836 and 1838 – in 1862. Thus, from the earliest of railway days, it could be said to have had an interest in the north-west in Cumberland and Westmorland. Strong commercial pressures brought the lines from the north-east into Westmorland over Stainmore and into Cumberland through the Tyne gap. All of them were taken into the North Eastern Railway company to become part of the LNER after 1924. NER routes into Cumbria were devastated by 1960s and 1970s closures.*

Brampton Junction, 1998. The rails on the first railway route into Cumbria from the north-east curve away towards the east passing the ruins of the Brampton Junction signal-box and the now derelict route to Alston (*see* p. 144). Hereabouts the colliery railways of the Earl of Carlisle experimented in rail transport from the late eighteenth century onwards, laying some of the earliest rails in the county.

NER trespass notice. The 40*s* penalty is the same as that on the Furness Railway notice on p. 61 but there is a softer and more explanatory approach from the North Eastern Railway.

Wetheral, July 1960. Originally produced in the 1920s for the Great Northern Railway these K3 class goods engines became very much part of the London & North Eastern Railway from amalgamation. Gresley 2–6–0 No. 61858 is here seen at Wetheral with a train of flat wagons.

Tebay, 1960. The 'special' train seen on p. 25 had a treat for the railway enthusiasts when the North Eastern Railway class Worsdell J21 0–6–0 British Railways No. 65033 was put on the turntable at Tebay. Built in 1889, this engine was first withdrawn in 1939 to be later put back in service and withdrawn finally in 1962 for preservation.

Carlisle, June 1961. The start of another west *v* east railway race? Ex-LNER Gresley V2 class 2–6–2 No. 60860 *Durham School* (*see also* p. 143 for this class of locomotive) appears set against 'Royal Scot' ex-LMS 4–6–0 No. 46108 *Seaforth Highlander* on the through lines at Citadel station, Carlisle.

Kingmoor Yard, Carlisle, 6 April 1963. North British Railway 'Glen' class D34 4–4–0 No. 256 *Glen Douglas* is seen on a 'Carlisle Rail Tour' excursion. Taken over by the LNER in 1923 as 9256, it was withdrawn from British Railways' service in 1959 as number 62469 when it was forty-six years old. It was restored to its North British condition and used for special tours for a number of years before being placed in the Glasgow Transport Museum.

Carlisle, August 1960. Ex-LNER Gresley J39 class 0–6–0 No. 64895 stands with passenger train at Carlisle station. In the background against the platform – but with one goods van in tow – is a Ministry of Supply-type engine, a Riddles 2–8–0 with BR No. 90168. This type of engine came directly out of the wartime requirement for heavy long-distance freight locomotives. Some of these engines were acquired by the LNER after the war but many more came into British Railways' hands later.

Carlisle, October 1960. Another of the great London & North Eastern steam locomotives was the Gresley A3 'Pacific' 4–6–2 express passenger engine, designed for the fastest trains on the east coast route to Scotland. Here in British Railways days is No. 60082 *Neil Gow* on the 'Thames–Clyde Express' on the west coast route.

Carlisle Canal, July 1960. A strange mixture on the Carlisle Canal sidings is the Gresley A3 'Pacific' No. 60089 *Felstead* with a goods van followed by what looks like a J39 0–6–0. The Canal siding at Carlisle came to the London & North Eastern railway from the North British Railway and continued, until closures in 1963 and 1969, to be the haunt of ex-LNER locomotives.

Carlisle Canal, July 1961. Looking very sad 'in store' at a Carlisle Canal sidings is Gresley A3 'Pacific' 4–6–2 No. 60079 *Bayardo*. A number of other 'dead' locomotives are sitting on the same siding.

Carlisle Canal, 22 July 1961. Class A4 'Pacific' 4–6–2 No. 60004 *William Whitelaw* was also on the Canal sidings. This LNER class of engine of the 1930s has been much written about. *Mallard* (60022) broke the world speed record for a steam engine at 126 mph. A number of the class have been preserved.

Kingmoor, Carlisle, September 1966. The end is obviously near as this very untidy ex-LNER A4 'Pacific' shows. No. 60026 *Miles Beevor* – with bits missing – stands besides BR 'Britannia' class 4–6–2 main line express engine No. 70047 (which is reported to have spent most of its ten or so years on the line between Holyhead and Euston).

Penrith station, 1 July 1952. The 10.30 a.m. Penrith to Darlington train at Penrith station. Ex-LMS-designe Ivatt 'Mogul' 2–6–0 No. 46481 heads the train at the platform. This class of locomotive was also built by BI and used by it for all types of work on this line. The North Eastern Eden Valley railway from Penrith ra through Clifton Junction to Appleby East station and then via Warcop to Kirkby Stephen East station where connected with the line over Stainmore. Before the days of BR, this was a LNER railway route (*see* als pp. 122 and 128). North-east holiday-making passengers could change at Penrith for the Keswick line but th route was used also by Eden Valley people visiting Penrith for shopping or changing at Penrith for the LNWI line north and south.

CHAPTER FOUR

FURNESS RAILWAY

Grange-over-Sands, August 1960. The ex-LMS 'Royal Scot' class 4–6–0 express passenger locomotive No. 46129 The Scottish Horse, *in its last years of service draws a train towards Arnside from Grange station. J. Richardson in his* Furness Past and Present *(1880) wrote, 'In the parliamentary session of 1844, powers were obtained by the Furness Railway Co. for the construction of their original line connecting the iron ore mines in the neighbourhood of Dalton and the slate quarries at Kirkby Ireleth with the sea coast at Barrow and Rampside.' Originally Ulverston was the intended terminus but this was not a popular idea with local landowners. The railway thus ended near Lindal. In 1845 the Whitehaven & Furness Junction Railway obtained permission to construct a line from Whitehaven to near to Kirkby Ireleth and the Furness Railway obtained permission to extend their lines to Ulverston and Broughton-in-Furness. The line from Ulverston to Lancaster was opened by the Ulverstone & Lancaster Railway Company in 1857 as the Furness Railway directors did not wish the two very expensive river crossings to be a burden on their company until the route was proven. The spectacular seaside embankment at Grange-over-Sands allowed passenger trains access to the village of Grange, which became a holiday resort with a promenade and ornamental gardens. Not everyone wanted such a development and Kendal architect George Webster, who – for health reasons – had just constructed the seaside Black Rock Villa only to find it cut off from the sea by the railway, instituted proceedings against the railway company.*

A Furness Railway advertising postcard of 1914. *The Illustrated Guide to The Holiday Resorts of the Furness Railway* (*c.* 1900) tells us 'The company provides a multiplicity of fortnightly, week-end, cheap day, market cheap day, cheap day with alternative return routes and special day tickets for anglers, golfers, tennis players, pleasure parties and the like with a magnificent series of circular tours by rail, coach and lake. The Company offers circular tours (by rail, coach and lake), a choice of 20 or more of these delightful circuits at almost absurdly low prices, the noted "6 lakes tour" being the most surprising value for money (13 shillings).'

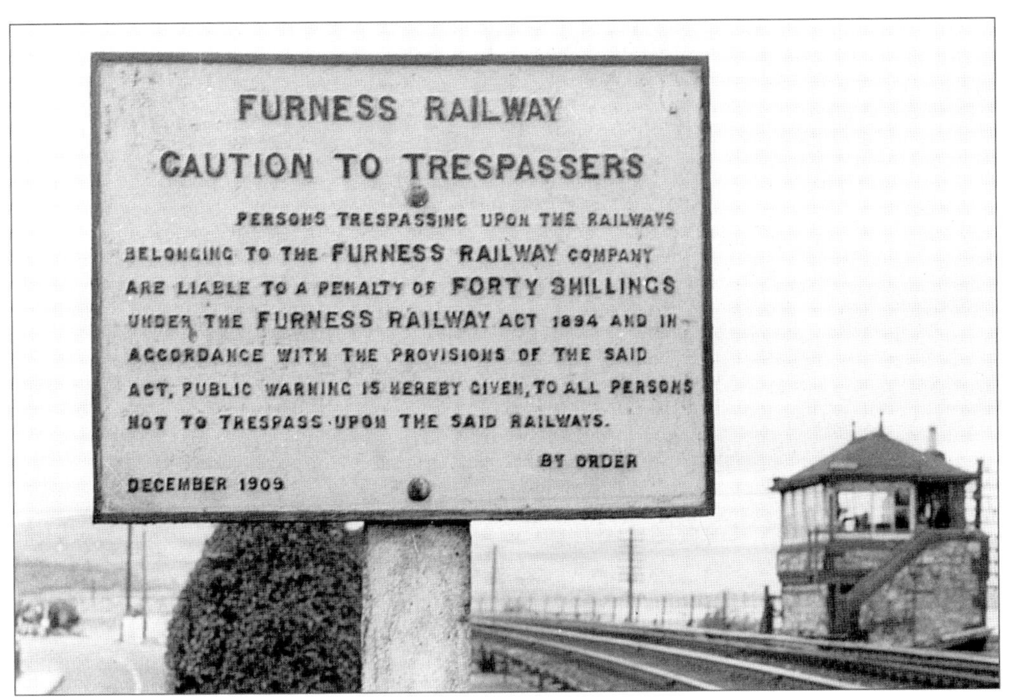

A Furness Railway notice near Arnside promenade. Notices of this sort are now much sought after by collectors. On the left is the Arnside promenade and behind the sign is the Kent estuary viaduct. It has been said that the railway transformed Arnside from 'a hamlet of almost impossible access' to Westmorland's only seaside resort. The pier and beachside road were built by the railway in an attempt to save Westmorland's only sea access as the nearby port of Milnthorpe had silted up after the railway was built.

Arnside station, *c.* 1910. A Barrow-bound passenger train about to be filled with schoolboys in their Eton collars pulls alongside the platform. 'Arnside occupies a convenient position on the Furness Railway 6 miles from Carnforth Junction rendering it a capital headquarters for tourists desirous of exploring the picturesque objects of interest in the Lake country.' (Furness Railway guide, 1900)

Arnside, 1923. FR 4–4–2 tank engine No. 39 on the Hincaster branch platform. This train was nicknamed 'Kendal Tommy'. (*See* p. 101 for more information on this now closed branch.)

Alfred Aslett with other railway officials inspecting the encasing of pillars at the Kent viaduct, 1915. The FR magazine explained, 'When cast iron is immersed in sea water for a considerable time change takes place in its composition and it is converted into a black substance resembling plumbago. The portions of the columns above the water line and buried in the bed of the river were not affected.'

Grange-over-Sands in the nineteenth century before the promenade was built. A FR guide says, 'In the immediate vicinity to the railway station what formerly was a piece of waste land has been tastefully laid out as a recreation ground with pleasant walks and an ornamental sheet of water surrounded by numerous shrubs and flowering plants.'

'Kirkland Scout at his table, 1913' was the title of this photograph, which was probably given on a suitable occasion by Alfred Aslett (*see* opposite), General Manager of the Furness Railway, to his chairman the Duke of Devonshire at Holker. The dog, seen here at Aslett's home, Stanyon Lodge, Ford Park, Ulverston, is pictured 'with "its" collection of thirty-eight albums, containing 18,000 postcards of dogs of all nations', according to the endorsement.

Grange-over-Sands sidings, 15 October 1960. 4MT 2–6–4T No. 42120 lets off steam while repairs are being carried out in Grange sidings (*see also* p. 74). Unfortunately no details of the incident have survived with the picture.

Grange-over-Sands, *c.* 1960. Ivatt 'Mogul' 2–6–0 No. 43026 with a branch passenger train passes under the footbridge as it leaves Grange station going towards Carnforth. This class of locomotive was introduced by the LMSR on the eve of nationalization.

Grange-over-Sands, 1900. Contrast the locomotive and carriages in this picture with the one above; FR class D3 0–6–0 No. 9 with a passenger train leaving Grange towards Kents Bank before the promenade was constructed. The engine was withdrawn by the LMSR in 1932.

Kents Bank station, July 1961. Ex-LMS Ivatt 'Mogul' 2–6–0 No. 43008 with a branch passenger train with passengers embarking bound for Cark and the Furness area. The FR guide states, regarding Kents Bank: 'It is noticeable as having been, before the construction of the railway, the point of starting and returning across the Sands.'

Cark station, 1880s. A Grange-bound Sharp, Stewart locomotive pulls a passenger train into Cark station in the late nineteenth century. The passenger line crossing can be seen in the centre of the station. A footbridge was installed in 1908. This is where the Duke of Devonshire, Chairman of the Furness Railway Company, would alight for his home at Holker nearby. What would he think of his station today?

Cark coal siding, August 1914. After Remount Department officers had scoured the countryside for horses, the acquisitions were assembled at various points before being put on to trains to travel to the Front. The Territorial Army had already gone off to France as the British Expeditionary Force and advertisements were being put in newspapers calling for more men and horses. The men were offered engagements lasting three years – or until the war ended (*see also* p. 98).

Cark station, 1920s. A flood in the station and yard has isolated the signal-box, which appears in connection with other disasters in the Furness Railway *Working Handbook Supplement, 1915* which advises, 'a wind pressure-gauge and recorder is fixed at the west end of the Leven viaduct and when the wind is of such a pressure as to make it dangerous for passenger trains to cross the viaduct, alarm bells will ring in the signal-boxes at Plumpton Junction, Ravensbarrow and Cark.'

Ulverston railway stations. The railway came to Ulverston from both directions with much difficulty. An Ac was passed allowing the Barrow line in 1846 but it did not reach Lindal until 1851 and Ulverston until 1854 The Ulverston–Lancaster line also proved difficult to construct because of the need to ford the Crake, Leve and Kent estuaries. It was finally opened in 1857. This heralded much tourist and other development in th North Lonsdale area. The new station (below) was designed by the Lancaster architects Paley and Austin an opened in 1874.

The Furness Railway.

List of Local Passenger Fares to . . . Ulverston . . .

Stations.	1st single		2nd single		3rd single		1st return		2nd return		*M'kt. return	
	s.	d.	s.	d.	s.	d.	s.	d.	s.	d.	s.	d.
Ambleside	3	10	2	9	2	3	5	10	4	4	3	5
Arnside	2	6	1	8	1	1	3	11	2	7	1	8
Askam	1	7	1	1	0	8	2	5	1	8	1	0
Barrow	1	10	1	3	0	9	2	10	1	11	1	2
Barrow, Ramsden Dock ...	1	11	1	4	0	10	3	0	2	0		
Bootle	5	0	3	4	2	2½	7	10	5	3	3	4
Bowness	3	4	2	3	1	9	4	10	3	4	2	8
Braystones	7	5	4	11	3	3	11	6	7	8	4	11
Broughton	2	10	1	11	1	2½	4	5	2	11	1	10
Cark	1	1	0	9	0	5½	1	8	1	2	0	9
Carnforth	3	7	2	5	1	6½	5	7	3	9	2	4
Coniston	4	6	3	0	1	11½	6	11	4	8	3	0
Dalton	0	11	0	7	0	4½	1	5	0	11	0	7
Drigg...	6	3	4	2	2	9	9	9	6	6	4	2
Eskmeals	5	7	3	9	2	5½	8	8	5	10	3	9
Foxfield	2	7	1	9	1	1½	4	0	2	8	1	9
Furness Abbey	1	2	0	10	0	6	1	10	1	3	0	9
Grange	1	11	1	3	0	9½	2	11	2	0	1	3
Greenodd	0	9	0	6	0	3½	1	1	0	9	0	6
Green Road	3	0	2	0	1	3½	4	7	3	1	2	0
Haverthwaite	1	3	0	10	0	6	1	11	1	3	0	9
Heversham	3	2	2	1	1	4½	4	11	3	3	2	1
Kents Bank	1	6	1	0	0	7½	2	4	1	7	1	0
Kirkby	2	2	1	6	0	11	3	5	2	3	1	5
Lindal	0	7	0	5	0	2½	0	11	0	7	0	4
Lake Side	1	10	1	3	0	9	2	10	1	10	1	2
Millom	3	5	2	4	1	6	5	4	3	7	2	3
Nethertown	7	8	5	1	3	4½	11	11	7	11	5	1
N. Lonsdale Level Crossing	0	6	0	4	0	2	0	9	0	6	0	3
Priory	0	8	0	6	0	3	1	1	0	8		
Ravenglass	5	11	3	11	2	7	9	2	6	1	3	11
Roose	1	6	1	0	0	7½	2	4	1	7	1	0
Sandside	2	10	1	11	1	3	4	5	2	11	1	11
St. Bees	8	2	5	6	3	7	12	9	8	6	5	5
Seascale	6	8	4	6	2	11	10	5	6	11	4	5
Sellafield	7	0	4	8	3	0½	10	10	7	3	4	7
Silecroft	4	1	2	9	1	9	6	4	4	2	2	8
Silverdale	3	0	2	0	1	3½	4	7	3	1	2	0
Torver	4	0	2	8	1	9	6	3	4	2	2	8
Whitehaven	9	0	6	0	3	11½	14	0	9	4	6	0
Woodland	3	4	2	3	1	5	5	2	3	5	2	2

* *Thursdays only.*

N.B.—Special Fares will be issued on Wednesday, July 15th, 1[illegible]—North Lonsdale Rose Show Day.

Fares to Ulverston. This late nineteenth-century table shows the Furness Railway fares for first-, second- and third-class passengers wishing to visit Ulverston. The market day special rate is of great interest – a passenger could save 9*d* on the second-class return fare from Barrow! The North Lonsdale level crossing entry on the short Conishead Priory branch indicates business from the nearby iron works (*see* over).

LONDON MIDLAND & SCOTTISH RAILWAYS

FROM THE

NORTH LONSDALE IRON & STEEL Co.,

LIMITED

Ulverston Hematite No. X

To SHEFFIELD, L. M. S. Railway.

Via Furness & Midland.

For

HY. BESSEMER & Co., Ltd.

Wagon No.............. Carriage Paid.

Weight.............Tons.........Cwt. Date.................192

The North Lonsdale Iron & Steel Company opened at Ulverston in 1874 adjacent to the Ulverston canal an by 1883 the FR had opened a branch line via the works through to Conishead Priory station. A mino tramline was also constructed to convey limestone for the blast furnaces from Gascow quarry. Passenger traffi to the Priory ceased in 1916. This goods wagon label is from the days of the London Midland & Scottis Railway in the 1920s shortly after the line's transfer from the Furness Railway. The Ulverston iron and stee works' first manager was William Tosh who was brought down from Maryport where he had been with th Solway Haematite Iron Company. He earned £1,000 a year 'paid quarterly' plus 2½ per cent commission. Th *Mannex Guide* of 1882 says, 'The Iron smelting works of the North Lonsdale Iron & Steel Company have no been in operation about six years and comprise four furnaces of the most modern type and of the large capacity in the Furness and Cumberland district. The company also possesses unrivalled facilities in its shippin pier adjoining the works for the distribution of its large brand of pig-iron to the various distant markets Historians tell us that the Ulverston Iron Works were also erected in 1874 as the start of the great financi depression, although no one noticed at the time. Four years after the start of production the combined iro and steel works in the Furness district were asking the Furness Railway for a reduction in tolls and, accordin to Dr J.D. Marshall in his *Furness and the Industrial Revolution*, 'fortunately the leading Furness Railwa Directors were also Iron Masters and a 7½ per cent reduction was granted.' The enterprise lasted with ups an downs until after the Second World War when it was closed and its site was taken over by Glaxo Laboratories.

Furness Railway rebuilt Sharp, Stewart class D1 0–6–0 No. 115 (above) was to become famous on 22 September 1892 when it sank into an iron ore mine subsidence beneath the Furness line at Lindal Bank. The driver and fireman scrambled to safety and for a while it appeared that the engine and tender could be saved, but further subsidence meant that only the tender was recovered. The engine has still not been recovered although speculation continues over the possibility. The picture below shows clearly the hole and damage to the adjoining tracks. The *Barrow Herald and Dalton Advertiser* of 1 November 1892 reported that the work in filling the hole was very successfully carried out. Nine huge baulks of timber each 36 ft long and 15 in square braced together by means of steel plates firmly bolted by 1¾ inch bolts formed a substantial bridge.

Dalton station at the turn of the century. Rule 92 of the 1916 *Rules and Regulations for the guidance of the officers and men in the service of the Furness Railway* declares: 'The stationmaster must daily inspect the station and see that the rooms, offices, closets, urinals, and platforms are kept neat and clean.' Hence the redecoration of the station canopy.

Accident at Dalton, *c.* 1900. Here we see a passenger train which has overriden the buffers at Dalton station. About two years earlier the *Barrow News* reported a narrow escape for a passenger train on 16 June 1898 where 20–30 breakaway coal wagons on the main line were about to run away from Dalton down the Lindal Bank. There was a passenger train in the Dalton siding with its engine detached. The nearby signalman diverted the wagons down the siding and at the same time shouted to the engine driver who drove towards the runaways, then reversed in time to intercept them and apply steam to finally stop them within 150 yards of commencing the emergency shunt. Meanwhile the stationmaster and a porter had boarded the wagons and applied the brakes. The *News* report added, 'All passengers who travel on the Furness Railway are aware of the steep gradient from Dalton to Lindal.'

ɜarrow-in-Furness station, before the Second World War. The photograph above is a general view of the ıterior. Note the litter on the line. The view below shows the WH Smith's bookstall, with headlines ıcluding 'Mussolini prepares for war'. Richardson in his *Furness Past and Present* (1880) says, 'The principal epot on this wonderful little line is Barrow, but how changed is the place since the first engine ran over the riginal system. A few wooden sheds sufficed for housing the 3 or 4 engines they possessed and the little vooden station, affording ample accommodation at the time, was in due course replaced by the commodious ne which now exists.'

A Furness Railway parcels van at Barrow, pre-1918. This early van bears the ever-present name of Alfred Aslett, who was the FR Company Secretary and General Manager from 1895 to 1918 (*see also* pp. 62–3).

Barrow-in-Furness motive power depot crane, 15 October 1960. The Barrow motive power depot was a legacy of the Furness Railway that survived well into British Railways' days. The depot used BR shed No. 11A. The crane is seen here on Grange-over-Sands siding hauled by 4MT 2–6–4T No. 42120. Another fine picture of this work being carried out – from Preston Whiteley's collection – can be found on p. 64.

The staff at Ramsden Dock station, Barrow. The FR branch from Buccleuch Junction to Ramsden dock opened in 1881. Passenger boat services were available to Fleetwood, Belfast and the Isle of Man. These were discontinued at the advent of the First World War but the railway station remained open until 1936.

Roa Island railway station, 1905. This postcard was inscribed: 'This station was taken from the watchhouse top by Uncle Dick.' This was one of the earliest portions of the FR lines and was opened to passengers in August 1846. Travellers from Fleetwood in those days came ashore at Piel pier adjoining this station.

Furness Railway steamer *Lady Moyra*, 1910. This paddle-steamer originally built as the *Gwalia* was renamed th *Lady Moyra* after the wife (inset) of Lord Richard Cavendish of Holker Hall. Withdrawn from the Furnes Railway in 1914, this steamer saw First World War service and then was renamed the *Brighton Queen*. Sh carried passengers along the Channel coast until she was sunk at Dunkirk in 1940. The crowded vessel is see below in a photograph by Edward Sankey taken on 11 August 1911 as she was carrying passengers on Barrow–Southport excursion.

The paddle-steamer *Lady Evelyn*, *c*. 1910. The *Lady Evelyn* was built on the Firth of Forth and came into FR service in 1901. She was named after the wife (inset) of Lord Victor Cavendish, chairman of the Furness Railway Company. The boat was so popular that she was extended in length by Vickers of Barrow in 1904. It was taken out of FR service in 1914 and after war service was renamed the *Brighton Belle*. She too was lost at Dunkirk in 1940. Below we see Sankey's photograph of a crowd on the boat *en route* from Fleetwood to Barrow on 9 September 1910.

FURNESS RAILWAY.

Popular Sea and Rail Excursions. ::

P.S. "LADY MARGARET."

For further information respecting the Sailings of the Steamers, apply to Mr. F. J. Ramsden, Superintendent of the Line, Barrow; at all Furness Railway Stations; also at any of Messrs. Thos. Cook & Son's Offices; and for conditions under which the tickets are issued, see detailed handbills.

ALFRED ASLETT, *Secretary and General Manager.*

DAILY (including Sundays) from WHITSUNTIDE until the end of SEPTEMBER,

The Furness Railway Company's Commodious and Fast Paddle Steamers,

"Lady Margaret" or "Lady Evelyn"

WILL SAIL DAILY (Weather and other unforeseen circumstances permitting) between

Barrow and Fleetwoo

(For BLACKPOOL).

Through Return Fares from Barrow to Blackpool

(Fleetwood to Blackpool by Rail)

Saloon and 1st Class, **4/6.** Fore Cabin and 3rd Class, **2/9**

FARES—Barrow and Fleetwood:

Saloon—Single, **2/6,** Return, **3/-,**
Fore Cabin—Single, **1/6,** Return, **2/-**

Tickets are also issued between **BARROW & BLACKPOO**

For Two Days, or from Friday or Saturday to the following Sunday, Monday or Tuesday, as follows:

Saloon and 1st Class, **5/9.** Fore Cabin and 3rd Class, **3/9.**

Weekly Tickets—Barrow and Fleetwood:

For **SEVEN** Return Journeys—Saloon, **10/-.** Fore Cabin, **6/-**

Season Tickets—Barrow and Fleetwood:

Saloon—One Month, £1 5s. Two Months, £1 12s. 6d.
For the Season, £2.

No Luggage Allowed.

Barrow-in-Furness, March, 1907.

Luncheons, Teas, and Refreshments provided on board by SPIERS & POND, Ltd.

A poster advertising the FR Barrow to Fleetwood boats available for the 1907 season. Alfred Aslett's name again prominent. His rules for the voyage include 'no luggage allowed'. The *Lady Margaret* was acquired by the FR in 1903 to assist the *Lady Evelyn* on this popular excursion. She was withdrawn from FR service in 190 when she was purchased by the Royal Navy. She was replaced by the paddle-steamer *Philomel*, affectionatel called the *Full of smell*. For further details see our *Around Barrow-in-Furness*, p. 17 (1993). Below, passengers ca be seen on the *Philomel en route* from Fleetwood to Barrow on 18 August 1908.

'The last special dinner car from Barrow-in-Furness'. Cynicus strikes at the Furness Railway in this postcard from the beginning of the twentieth century pointing out, no doubt, that most trains from Barrow did not carry a dining car.

THIS PORTION OF THE SHEET TO BE RETAINED BY THE PROPRIETOR

Furness Railway Company. No. S.1586

DIVIDEND STATEMENT.

SECRETARY'S OFFICE,
BARROW-IN-FURNESS, *August 28th, 1916.*

I beg to inform you that the Directors, having declared an Interim Dividend on the Consolidated Ordinary Stock of the Company at the rate of £2 per cent. per annum for the first half of the year 1916, have resolved that the same be paid, together with the
half-yearly Dividend on the Consolidated Guaranteed and the several Preference Stocks of the Company, to the Proprietors who were
registered at the closing of the Transfer Books on the 29th ultimo, and I am instructed to send you the following Statement and Draft
for the Dividend so payable. I hereby certify that I have deducted for Income Tax the amount set forth in this Statement, and that the
sum so deducted will be paid by me to the proper Officer for the receipt of Taxes. Proprietors requiring repayment of Income Tax are
informed that the Inland Revenue Office will receive this Statement as a Voucher in respect of claims which should be made after April
6th next.

ALFRED ASLETT, Secretary.

AMOUNT OF STOCK. £	Half-yearly Dividend to June 30th, 1916.	DIVIDEND. £	s.	d.
	Consolidated Guaranteed Stock, at 4 per cent. per annum.			
	Consolidated Preference Stock, at 4 ,, ,, ,,			
	Preference Stock, A .... at 4 ,, ,, ,,			
	Preference Stock, B .... at 4 ,, ,, ,,			
	Preference Stock, 1894 .... at 4 ,, ,, ,,			
	Preference Stock, 1899 .... at 4 ,, ,, ,,			
200	Consolidated Ordinary Stock ...at 2 per cent. per annum........	2	.	.
Name *Eleanor Hughes*	TOTAL DIVIDEND........	2	.	.
	Less Income Tax at 4s. 6d. in the £	.	9	.
	(The average rate for the year 1916, viz :— 3 months at 3s. 0d., and 9 months at 5s. 0d.) £	1	11	.

** N.B.—Proprietors are requested to give the Secretary early notice of any change of residence.

FR dividend statement, August 1916. The capital of the Furness Railway Company rose rapidly in the middle of the nineteenth century: originally £75,000 in the 1840s it had become £5,608,566 by the end of 1876. During the First World War the FR prospered. Dividends increased to 2 per cent in 1915 and the company was able to purchase £50,000 of war loan in the following year.

Furness Railway.

Circular
G.M. 182.

—:o:—

SECRETARY AND GENERAL MANAGER'S OFFICE,
BARROW-IN-FURNESS,
JANUARY 26TH, 1917.

ENLISTMENT OF RAILWAY EMPLOYEES IN THE VOLUNTEER FORCE.

—:o:—

I have pleasure in informing you that arrangements have been completed with the War Office for the enrolment of Railway Employees in the Volunteer Force.

Members of the Furness Railway Company's Staff who desire to enlist in the Volunteer Force will be drafted into a special Section known as Section " R," the intention being that any members enlisted in this Section will not be called out for actual Military Service without the Company's consent.

Commencing forthwith any member of the Staff or Employee of the Company who wishes to join the Volunteer Force is at liberty to do so under the Regulations laid down in Army Council Instruction No. 66 of 1917, an extract of which is enclosed herewith.

It must be understood that the Company are under no obligation to release the men from their Railway duties for the purpose of attending drills. At the same time every encouragement will be given to the men to attend drills in their own time in order that they may make themselves proficient for carrying out their duties with the Volunteer Force in case they can be spared from Railway work when an emergency arises.

Full particulars may be obtained from the various Volunteer Headquarters as to the regulations which will apply to the Volunteer Force generally and which regulations will have to be complied with.

In connection with Section " R " of the Volunteer Force it is proposed to form a special Sub-Section for Railwaymen who will be employed in emergency in the zone of operations.

THIS SUB-SECTION FOR RAILWAYMEN WILL INCLUDE:—

(1) Men attached to Armoured Trains.

(2) Railway Telegraph Linesmen who are specially told off for the purpose of assisting and directing in the destruction of telegraph and telephone lines in case of an emergency.

Certain Railway Officials will be given commissions in the Volunteer Force for duty with this Special Sub-Section, and some of the men in it will be made Non-Commissioned Officers. The Non-Commissioned Officers and men in this Sub-Section will have to sign a special agreement for the period of the War. They will be provided with uniform, either from Public or Railway Funds as may be subsequently determined, but as far as Military duty goes, will in normal times only be required to appear in uniform (say) once a month before their respective Officers, who will be the Railway Officials referred to above.

In the event of the Volunteers being called out for actual Military Service, this Sub-Section will also be called out and will be employed solely on their special technical duties.

Furness Railway circular G.M. 182, 1917. While the railway may have been prosperous during the First World War, staffing was obviously a problem as men disappeared to the services. This circular was issued by Alfred Aslett on 26 January 1917 explaining that 'the arrangements have been completed with the War Office'.

Circular
G.M. 184.

Furness Railway.

Secretary and General Manager's Office,
BARROW-IN-FURNESS,
January 23rd, 1917.

CULTIVATION OF LAND FOR FOOD SUPPLY.

——:o:——

In order to utilise to the greatest possible extent the Railway Company's spare land for the purpose of the production of Food, and thus assist the Food Supply of the Country, the Company invite applications from their Staff and Employees, and from members of the Public, for the use, during the War, of vacant strips of land both inside and outside the Railway fences.

Exceptional terms have been arranged which will provide for about 300 square yards of land at an annual rent of 1s. About 400 plots are already rented by Employees and the Public, and it is hoped that the present tenants will be induced to cultivate more vacant strips.

The Allotments are only to be used for growing vegetables for food which do not continue productive for more than a year.

Application should be made to the nearest Station Master, or to the Secretary.

Please make these arrangements known to your Staff and the Public, and acknowledge receipt on the annexed form.

ALFRED ASLETT,
SECRETARY & GENERAL MANAGER

....

....

Furness Railway.

.... *Station.*

January .... 1917.

CULTIVATION OF LAND FOR FOOD SUPPLY.

I beg to acknowledge receipt of your Circular G.M. 184 *of the* 23*rd instant, which has my special attention.*

....

To the General Manager,
Furness Railway,
Barrow-in-Furness.

FR circular G.M. 184, 1917. Paradoxically this was issued three days before 182! FR land inside and outside railway fences was offered for cultivation to support the government's food supply scheme. Note that Mr Aslett would not permit any vegetable with a life span of more than one year to be grown.

Kirkby-in-Furness and Askam stations. Kirkby station is seen before 1907 with the staff posing on the platform. The card was posted on the Carnforth to Whitehaven travelling railway post-office. Below, the 3-mile Kirkby to Askam railway journey humour card requests that passengers do not to pick the flowers while riding in the train! Askam of course did not exist before the iron works and railway station were opened in 1867/8.

Foxfield station, *c.* 1900. A FR motor unit of three carriages stands at the Coniston platform. Prior's *Guide* says, 'Foxfield Junction occurs after a run of about half an hour from Barrow. Passengers for Coniston generally change here after which a further run of 25 min. deposits you at the terminus immediately under the Old Man. It should be, moreover, remarked that Broughton, the first station on this branch line is the place to start from on a survey of the Duddon valley by hiring a car if you are not good for a twenty miles' walk.'

Foxfield Junction, December 1957. 'Royal Scot' class ex-LMS 4–6–0 No. 46151 *The Royal Horse Guardsman* with a south-bound Euston express. Richardson's *Furness Past and Present* (1880) informs us that, 'This section (of railway) is about 34 miles in length and runs from Foxfield to Whitehaven. Powers for the construction of this line were obtained in 1845 and it was opened through in November 1850.' (*See* p. 117 for the now closed branch to Coniston.)

Millom station, *c.* 1905. Until the advent of the Furness Railway, Millom was a small isolated community centred around the church and castle. The present town was developed in the 1860s after the discovery of one of the largest deposits of iron in the world at Hodbarrow. Later, blast furnaces were built and the railway station changed its name from Holborn Hill to Millom.

Eskmeals station, *c.* 1900. The three Furness Railway stations between Millom and Ravenglass were Silecroft, Bootle and Eskmeals. In 1900 it was recorded that the post office was at Bootle station. William Hodgson was postmaster, Matthew Henry Gribble was the stationmaster and Charles Marsh was stationmaster at Eskmeals with Thomas Wilson at Silecroft. Eskmeals was then famous for its large rabbit warrens in the sand dunes. It was also the home of the Vickers & Co. gun range, which still exists and was originally used for testing battleship guns from the Barrow works.

Ravenglass, 1960. The Cumbrian rail tour of 4 September 1960 allowed time for photographs at Ravenglass station when the ex-LMS Fowler 'Patriot' class 4–6–0 No. 45503 *The Royal Leicestershire Regiment* was at the head of the train.

Ravenglass, *c.* 1900. In complete contrast to the top picture is this view of a small group of adults and children admiring the Furness Railway Sharp, Stewart 0–6–0 No. 92 on the siding at Ravenglass (*see also* p. 92). The photograph is taken from the south and shows the station buildings on the left. In recent years they have been transformed into the pub called the Ratty Arms, named after the Ravenglass & Eskdale Railway – 'La'al Ratty' (*see* over).

The Ravenglass & Eskdale Railway. In 1875 this 3-ft gauge track opened as a mineral railway moving iro ore with some passenger traffic from Boot to the main line at Ravenglass. Above is Beckfoot halt with i passenger shelter and below, one of the rickety trains can be seen at the Boot terminus in 1905. There wer also halts at Muncaster and Eskdale Green. The company was bankrupt in 1908 and the line became derelic until it was rescued and became a 15-in miniature railway during the First World War. One of the firs engines was the *Sans Pareil*, built by well-known railway modeller, Mr W.J. Bassett-Lowke (*see als* p. 33). Both photographs date from the days of the original 3-ft gauge line.

urness Railway engine No. 1 was an Aspinall design class D5 0–6–0 and was of a type normally used on the ancashire & Yorkshire Railway. Above, it can be seen in the condition in which it was delivered in Furness ailway livery in 1913. It was taken over in 1923 by the LMSR as 12494 and with yet another number ange to 52494 we see it below with BR, in the late 1940s, at Workington shed. It carries the shed code 12D f Kirkby Stephen. The engine was withdrawn in 1956.

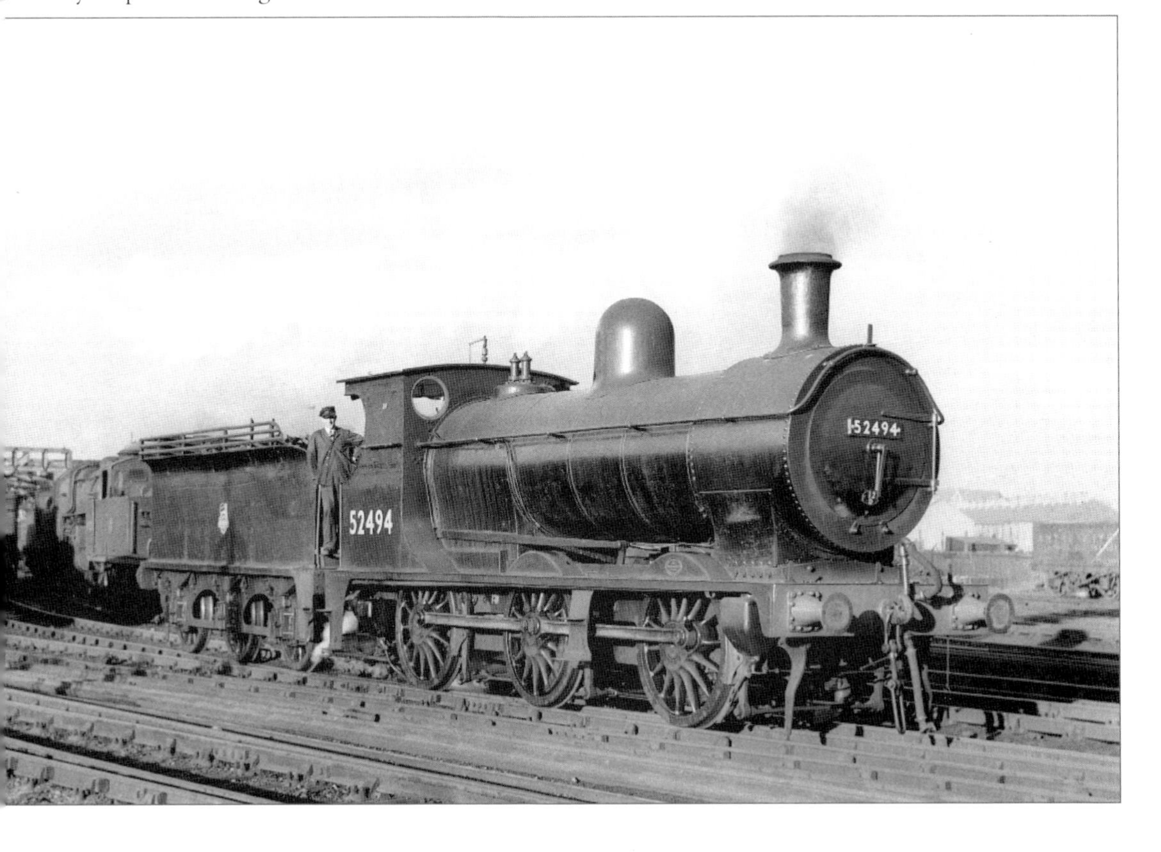

ALL RATES AND CHARGES are to be paid on delivery of the Goods unless the Consignee has a Ledger Account with th Company, which is granted upon the following, amongst other conditions: that the amount of the Account as rendered is remitte within Eight days thereafter to the Station from which received. Errors or overcharges, when found to exist, will be at onc rectified and allowed in next settlement, but shall form no ground for delay or deduction in payment of Accounts.

The Company cannot accept reference to Senders or a third party for carriage.

(531-6/17) CHEQUES TO BE DRAWN TO THE ORDER OF THE LONDON AND NORTH WESTERN RAILWAY COMPANY, AND CROSSED & Co

Please to require a Printed Stamped Receipt for Amounts of £2, and upwards.

Messrs The W'haven United Gas Co Whitehaven STATION, Oct. 16th 192

TO THE LONDON AND NORTH WESTERN RAILWAY COMPANY

DATE.		Invoice No.	From or To.	STATION.	SENDER OR CONSIGNEE. 574	SPECIES AND MARKS.	WEIGHT. T. C. Q. lbs.	Rate.	Paid on.	TOTAL. £ s. d.
Oct.	12	372	To	Workington	J. Rubery & Sons	1 c/s Fittgs. 1 Manhole Lid	1 0 10	6/4		1 8
"	13	433		Edinburgh	Alder McKay	1 Box cookg. meter	1 2	35/2		3 2
										4 10

Complications at Whitehaven goods station, 1920. Two invoices – one for the Furness, and the other for th London & North Western Railway companies – both issued to the Whitehaven United Gas Company shov the difficulties experienced in deciding which railway company would receive payment when there were s many involved in work locally. Companies operating in the Whitehaven area included: the Furness; London & North Western; Maryport & Carlisle; Cleator & Workington Junction; Cockermouth, Keswick & Penrith; an Whitehaven, Cleator & Egremont Junction railways.

1084. 2,000 | 9 | 19.

NOTICE.—When Carriage is charged forward on Goods said to have been bought "Carriage Paid," this Company will not undertake to rectify unless proof is produced that Sender HAS ACTUALLY PAID the amount.

WHITEHAVEN GOODS Station, Nov. 20th 1920

Messrs The Whitehaven Gas Co. 949.

To the Furness Railway Company, Dr.

If the amount is remitted by Cheque or P.O. Order, it should be made payable to the FURNESS RAILWAY COMPANY.
Receipt Stamp printed "Received for F.R. Co." to be given for £2 and upwards.

Invoice Pro. No.	Date.		Sender or Consignee.	Description of Goods.	From	To	Paid on. s. d.	Weight. Tons. cwts. qrs. lbs.	Rate.	£ s. d.
543.	Nov.	12	Cannon & Gaskins	1 Pkge Cty Stocks		Deepfields		2 0	2/10	1 5
7	"	"	J. Milne & Sons	1 Cty Box.		Leeds		2 0	2/4	1 2
669	"	15	Edwards Bros.	1 " "		B'gham		2 0	2/10	1 5
687	"	16	G. Glover Ltd.	1 " "		Manchester		2 0	2/4	1 2
373	"	1		1 c/s Gas Fittgs.	B'gham			3 0	40/-	5 3
608	"	12		1 Pcl. Files	Sheffield			12	32/4	2 4
										£ 12 9

Whitehaven Bransty station, just after the Second World War. Ex-Furness Railway Pettigrew class D5 0–6–0 (FR No. 28) with BR No. 52499 in British Railways days in the late 1940s or early 1950s, pulling out of Whitehaven Bransty station. The engine had survived from 1914 and was not withdrawn by BR until 1957, the last of the original FR class. The coal mines of the west coast are still visible in this photograph. The line from Maryport had reached here as early as 1847 and extended to the harbour (on the right) in 1848. In 1852 a tunnel from Corkickle, where the Furness Railway terminated, was brought through to Bransty.

Bird's-eye view of Harrington station. W.G. Collingwood, in his *Lake Counties* guide of 1902 describes Harrington as 'a seaport and LNWR station'. The line was opened as part of the Whitehaven Junction Railway in 1847. Evidence of intensive coastal industrialization can be seen in this photograph.

Workington, July 1963. Class 4F ex-Midland Railway Fowler 0–6–0 No. 44065 at Workington sheds. This picture was taken only five years before the end of steam on British Railways. In 1966 the Cockermouth, Keswick & Penrith Railway – which extended to Workington – was closed from Keswick westwards (*see* 'Closed Lines', p. 135).

The 'Last Train Home', *c.* 1900. Siddick was quoted as the extreme end of the Furness Railway. The company had many problems reaching so far north and had constant difficulties working with the many other organizations in the area. The postcard was barbed in its humour – the service appears anything but express.

CHAPTER FIVE

MARYPORT & CARLISLE RAILWAY

Smellie Maryport & Carlisle 2–4–0 No. 10 is seen at Currock sheds, Carlisle, c. 1900. Only three of these engines were built in the mid-1870s for the Maryport & Carlisle (M&C); they carried Nos 8, 10 and 13 and all were still in service in 1923 when the amalgamations took place but were almost immediately withdrawn. The M&C was opened in 1845 but had difficulty competing with the Lancaster & Carlisle Railway and the Caledonian Railway to obtain a terminus at Carlisle. At one stage the M&C's temporary station was taken down overnight by the Lancaster & Carlisle workmen! Eventually, in 1851 the M&C became users-by-agreement at Citadel station. The Currock engine sheds and sidings were opened in 1876 when the company moved their facilities from the original shed by the junction at Bogfield. The Currock sheds were closed in 1923 when rationalization of Carlisle's railway facilities was carried out.

Buck Hill, near Great Broughton, *c.* 1900. The Bullgill to Brigham branch of the Maryport & Carlisle Railway had a junction at Linefoot with the Cleator & Workington Junction Railway (C&W) (*see* p. 155). Here what looks remarkably like Furness Railway Sharp, Stewart 0–6–0 No. 92 is seen with a passenger train on C&W rails (*see also* p. 85).

Brigham Junction. A Maryport & Carlisle Railway train is seen in the bay at Brigham station (*see also* p. 141). The Maryport & Carlisle ran to Bullgill and then on to its main line. It shared Brigham Junction station with the Workington to Cockermouth, Keswick and Penrith traffic.

Maryport station. The headquarters of the Maryport & Carlisle Railway were at Maryport station. Part of the once grand buildings that housed the station and offices can be seen in this photograph of an M&C 2-4-0 standing at the platform (there was only one). In recent years Maryport's modern station has become little more than a 'bus stop' between Barrow and Carlisle.

Maryport, 20 Sept 1909

The Glasgow & South Western Rly Co.

To the MARYPORT AND CARLISLE RAILWAY COMPANY. Dr.

1909							
Aug 31	To Amount of Toll for use of Railway to Engine Sheds at Currock Carlisle in accordance with Agreement, viz:-			d			
	Engines	No	2097	6	52	8	6
	Carriages	"	279	2	2	6	6
	Wagons	"	162	1		17	.
	Coal & Stores	Tons	1559	1	6	9	11
					£62	11	11

Paid Oct 16 J.W.

(286)

MARYPORT AND CARLISLE RAILWAY.

AUDIT OFFICE,
MARYPORT,

Statement of Proportion due to the London & North Western Company
in respect of Mineral Traffic for the Month of December 1911.

McCorquodale & Co. Limited, Printers, Glasgow and London.

COLLIERY.	DESTINATION.	Description.	Wagons.	Route.	Tons.	Cwts.	Rate.	£	s.	d.
Blayton No 4 Pit	Clibrun N.E.	Coal	L.T.	Carlisle & Penrith	6	2	2/5		14	9
West Wylam N.E.	Cockermouth	Coke	"	Carlisle	5	6	4		1	9
					11	8			16	6

E & O.E.
John Shipper

(286)

MARYPORT AND CARLISLE RAILWAY.

AUDIT OFFICE,
MARYPORT,

Statement of Proportion due to the Furness Company
in respect of Mineral Traffic for the Month of December 1911.

McCorquodale & Co. Limited, Printers, Glasgow and London.

COLLIERY.	DESTINATION.	Description.	Wagons.	Route.	Tons.	Cwts.	Rate. Wagon hire d	£	s.	d.
Alice Pit Linefoot	Maryport	Coal	Hire	Linefoot	92	1	2		15	4
	Wigton	.	.	.	5	3	4		1	9
	Dearham	,	,	,	11	.	1			11
	Brigham	.	.	.	5	6	1			5
					113	10			18	5

E & O E
J Shipper

JM 29/6

laryport & Carlisle accounting. This group of accounts (*see also* opposite) illustrates the difficulties and greements that a small railway like the Maryport & Carlisle had to endure to make use of its assets. Accounts the Glasgow & South Western Railway Company, the London & North Western Railway Company and ne Furness Railway Company showed that there was little competition in the pre-First World War years. The ilasgow & South Western Railway were being billed for the use of the Currock sheds at Carlisle, the London North Western for mineral traffic from the west coast to local stations at Cockermouth and Cliburn, and the urness Railway for very similar traffic to very local stations at Maryport, Wigton, Dearham and Brigham! In ase someone had missed something the last two accounts were clearly marked 'E & OE' (errors and omissions xcepted). The difficulties and duplications in providing a railway service in a very small area are underlined in hese three accounts from a system that would only be replaced following the amalgamations to form the LMS ailway Company and later British Railways. It is hard to imagine that anyone could wish to bring such red ape back into the railway service.

Barrow-in-Furness, 1920s. The takeover of the M&C by the London Midland & Scottish Railway in 1923 meant that many engines went straight to the scrapheap. Here a group of Maryport & Carlisle 0–6–0 engines are seen at Barrow-in-Furness, directly after the amalgamation, in the process of being dismantled.

Carlisle, 1950s. Ex-Midland Railway and LMS Fowler 2P 4–4–0 No. 40694 showing shed code 12D for Kirkby Stephen (ex-LNER) stands at the head of the train for Workington on the ex-Maryport & Carlisle line. All the old difficulties of a system based on myriad private companies seemed to have been resolved for ever.

CHAPTER SIX

CLOSED LINES MISCELLANY

THE LITTLE NORTH WESTERN – KIRBY LONSDALE TO LOWGILL

Sedbergh station, c. 1910. Passengers and light goods await the arrival of the Ingleton-bound passenger train. Note the highly polished milk churns and the live calf in a sack. Sedbergh station continued in use after the withdrawal of ordinary passenger traffic in 1954 as a station for public school special trains and remained operational until about the time of the closure of the goods yard in 1964. The Little North Western was partially opened in 1861 as the Ingleton branch, from Lowgill, of the London & North Western Railway. It met the Midland Railway at Ingleton where both lines had a station. It was not until a year or so later that the Midland Railway was able to run through-trains from London. The problems that the London & North Western Railway caused these Midland Railway through trains from London to Glasgow (they were in competition) resulted in the 1876 opening of the Midland Railway's Settle–Carlisle line (see Chapter Two). Difficulties such as this were finally resolved through amalgamation into the LMS and nationalization in 1947. The wave of closures of goods yards saw the end of the line in 1966.

Kirkby Lonsdale station yard, August 1914. The advent of the First World War caused much railway traffic as men, animals and goods made their way to the Front. The image created by 1st West Lancs Field Ambulance 'Entraining for Mobilisation' was repeated all over the country and put on to postcards by official photographers as part of the publicity campaign for the war effort (*see also* p. 67).

Kirkby Lonsdale station, February 1963. Kirkby Lonsdale's station was nearly 2 miles from the small town and was just inside Lancashire. The wartime picture at the top of the page was taken in its heyday; this photograph comes from the last years of the line. Regular passenger services ceased in 1954 and the goods station at Kirkby Lonsdale was to be closed in 1964. The February snow reflects the station's bleak future.

Barbon station, July 1961. 'Situated on the banks of the River Lune amid scenery as varied and as beautiful as that of many of the most lauded spots on the Continent . . . the LNWR runs through the district . . . Stationmaster William Brennan' – this was the description of Barbon in a 1905 guidebook. Here it is seen in its declining years, a closed passenger station but a well-used goods line.

Middleton station, July 1961. This station was opened with the line in 1861 but suffered an early closure in April 1931. As can be seen the platforms had been swept away and the house left as a private residence by 16 July 1961.

Sedbergh station, 20 May 1962. Rerouting for a number of reasons from both the North Western and Midland main lines brought traffic on to the Little North Western. This is the Down 'Thames-Clyde Express' hauled by Type 4 'Peak' No. D75 roaring north through Sedbergh station.

Lowgill Junction, September 1965. The line was also a route for specials. On 4 September 1965 the north-bound railway enthusiasts' special was hauled by the famous ex-LNER Gresley-designed A3 'Pacific' 4–6–2 No. 60103 *Flying Scotsman.* (Note the use of the original number 4472 following restoration in 1963). The engine was designed for the main line expresses of the LNER route from London to Scotland, and to have *Flying Scotsman* in Cumbria and running over the Lowgill Junction was a moment to savour. The Little North Western line closed in July 1966 and Lowgill Junction disappeared.

'Grange to Kendal and back in one day' was the usual use for the Furness branch to the main line at Hincaster. It was for many years a useful and easy way to go shopping in Kendal and market day special tickets were offered. The Cynicus Company typically targeted branch lines such as this for their popular humour postcards.

Arnside, *c.* 1923. A Furness Railway class D3 0–6–0 engine No. 16 pulls a goods train on to the Hincaster branch. The goods trains on this route offered a useful service to both the north and north-east as well as providing a local goods service. This photograph dates from the times of the amalgamation with the LMS Railway during which this engine was renumbered 12477.

The cutting at Sandside survives to this day as an empty shell with the line removed. The branch from Arnsid to Hincaster Junction (*see* p. 107) on the London & North Western main line was opened in June 187 following the search for a route to transport coke and iron between the north-east and the Barrow area Originally only passenger traffic used the route, and the coke and iron trains continued via the difficul junction at Carnforth until the needs of the First World War effort demanded a revision of the arrangemen that kept goods off the branch. Between 1918 and 1939 the line continued to be used by passengers and good trains, until the Second World War saw the closure of local passenger services. The demise of iron and stee manufacture in Furness and of railway use in general brought about the branch's closure in September 1963 However, a line to the Sandside quarry was left in place until it too was closed in 1971. Parts of the rout alongside the Kent estuary are now a footpath and others have been lost under new development, but ther are plans to reopen some of the line.

Sandside station, 1920s. A lime works train on double track at Sandside. The signal box is on the platform en (*see* opposite for an earlier contrast).

andside station. Above, photographers Sawyers of Kendal recorded a neat Sandside station in about 1910 with single track and the signal-box on the quarry side of the line. Note the extensive goods siding. In 1966 below) Preston Whiteley recorded the station's last days as a quarry siding with a double line; the signal-box urvived on a new site on the station side of the line (*see* p. 102) but there was a building site where the station self used to be. The Paley and Austin-designed railway station was being replaced with concrete block flats of he ugly 'modern' design typical of the mid-1960s.

Sandside, *c.* 1930. Ex-Maryport & Carlisle Railway 0–6–0 locomotive on the Tebay to Barrow coke train o the Hincaster branch between Dallam viaduct and Sandside station. A number of the Maryport & Carlis engines are known to have been found jobs on the LMS after the 1923 amalgamation. Others wer scrapped (*see* p. 96).

Dallam bridge, 1930s. A railside view of the bridge over the River Bela at Dallam Park looking in th direction of Heversham. This magnificent bridge blocked the estuary end of Dallam Park and was part of th reason for the closure of the 'port' of Milnthorpe in the nineteenth century as the estuary silted up.

Dallam bridge from Haverbrack, 1930s. In this view the full extent of the river crossing can be seen. Heversham is on the right approached through a cutting and Sandside on the left approached by the Dixies embankment. The twenty-five arch bridge was erected in the 1870s.

Dallam bridge under demolition, 1966. The Hincaster branch was closed to through traffic in 1963 and the Dallam bridge was destroyed in 1966. Preston Whiteley, alert to the historic importance of the destruction, photographed the contractors at work in May 1966 as the metal three-span central section was taken down. South Cumbria lost an important and impressive structure, and the present discussion on reopening this useful branch has been left with a very big physical obstacle – which is probably exactly what was intended.

Heversham station. The picture above, taken in around 1910, shows a modest station in a cutting against the A6 road. There was a waiting-room and ticket office. From the late nineteenth century through to the 1930s the station was used by passengers wishing to connect with main line trains at both Oxenholme and Arnside as well as by Kendal shoppers. Preston Whiteley's picture below shows the scene in February 1960, with the station building demolished following the withdrawal of passenger services.

Hincaster Junction, 4 August 1962. At this point the line from Arnside joined the main line. A Type 4 English Electric diesel No. D374 drawing an Up passenger express train shows that these were changing times at the junction. The main Lancaster to Carlisle line was to undergo even greater changes with electrification in the 1970s. The view south from the junction signal box can be seen below on 5 August 1962.

'The Last Train to Greenodd'. Branch line humour again in this Cynicus postcard from around 1900. It is very unlikely that there would ever have been a great demand to be on the last train to Greenodd from Ulverston or anywhere on the branch.

Ulverston station, 1963. Type 2 diesel No. D5708 is seen at the head of the 4.10 p.m. train to Lakeside on 24 August 1963 (*see also* p. 112). Preston Whiteley, aware of the forthcoming line closure, here as elsewhere recorded the final days of the line.

Greenodd station, 1930s, with a goods train bound for Lakeside (above) and the railbridge over the Leven (below), *c.* 1910. The Greenodd line was first used for transport to and from the blast furnace at Backbarrow but carried tourists after the extension to Lakeside was opened in 1869. The double track from Ulverston and Plumpton Junction became a single line at Greenodd. The whole of the station and the viaduct were destroyed to become part of the route of the Greenodd bypass road which has covered the site completely since 1982.

Haverthwaite station, *c.* 1905. Haverthwaite provided the link for freight to and from Backbarrow ironworks, Lowwood gunpowder works and other industries associated with the water power available from the River Leven. The station was built when the branch line was opened to Lakeside pier in 1869. The goods yard and station are now the centre of the Lakeside & Haverthwaite preserved railway.

Newby Bridge station, *c.* 1918. Class G5 0–6–0 tank engine No. 21 draws a train alongside the platform.

Opposite: Runaway goods train smash at Haverthwaite. July 1932. The *North Western Daily Mail* of 16 July 1932 said: 'An alarming accident on Friday afternoon on the Lakeside branch of the LM&SR which might have resulted in serious loss of life but happily no one was injured. An engine was pushing about ten wagons and drawing two others from Haverthwaite station to Backbarrow ironworks. The train had to proceed up a steep gradient and when it nearly reached the top the engine came to a standstill. The weight of the wagons in front began to force back the engine and the other two wagons and owing to the greasy state of the rails and the sharp incline, the engine was powerless to pull up. The train gathered speed and careered down the incline for about half a mile, when, on nearing Haverthwaite station, the two wagons now in front of the engine collided with the stop blocks which were torn up and crashed through a wall on to the main road. The wagons tilted up right across the roadway which was completely blocked. One was a powder wagon but empty. Just prior to the crash a motor bus had pulled up a few yards away to discharge passengers but for which there would have been a terrible collision involving serious loss of life. No one was hurt and the engine driver and fireman jumped clear just in time. An electric pole was demolished – electricity supply to Backbarrow was cut off. It was after midnight before the road was cleared.'

Lakeside station, 24 August 1963. Type 2 diesel locomotive No. D5708 is seen with the 3.20 p.m. train to Ulverston. Two years later passenger services on the line to Lakeside were withdrawn and it was fully closed in 1967 (*see* p. 108).

The buffer stops inside Lakeside station, 1963. The interior of Lakeside station before the closure was very different from its appearance today as an uncovered platform nearly surrounded by car parking. Rail passengers originally disembarked from the Windermere lake steamers at Newby Bridge and boarded the train there. Since the River Leven was narrow and shallow at that point, the rail line was extended to a purpose-built station and quay at Lakeside which allowed the use of larger boats.

Lakeside station, *c.* 1910. The London & North Western Railway *Holiday Guide* of the period says: 'thence to Lake Side station, when passengers embark upon the steamers for Storrs Pier, the Ferry, Bowness, Lowwood and Ambleside. The station at Lake Side has a pavilion or covered balcony in which luncheons and teas are served and music is to be heard daily in the summer months. The landing stage adjoins the platform.'

Lakeside, *c.* 1900. The Furness Railway steam yacht *Swan* (I) is seen disembarking passengers at the Lakeside quay. The narrow gauge track that can be seen was for the transport of coal from the coalyard (in the middle of the present car park) which was served by the branch line. The narrow gauge track ran to the boats, with the crew members using a bogie wagon and swill baskets to get the coal aboard.

The *Tern* in Bowness Bay, *c.* 1909. This steamer was a twin-screw 'puffer' built in 1891 by Forrest of Wivenhoe, Essex. The steam engine was replaced by a diesel after the Second World War by British Railways which acquired her from the LMS railway company. She continues to ply the route between Ambleside and Lakeside, having had several recent changes of ownership and much refitting.

The *Cygnet* off Lakeside, 1908. Built by the Barrow Shipbuilding Company in 1879 she served the Furness then LMS railways. She was fitted with a diesel engine in 1924 and later sold into private ownership, sailing on Windermere for a number of years.

he steam yacht *Swan* arriving at Ambleside pier, 1908. The *Swan* (I) was a fast, twin-propellered steamboat uilt by T.B. Seath & Co. of Rutherglen in 1869: her construction coincided with the opening of the ation and quay at Lakeside. She was dismantled in 1938. *Swan II*, a modern diesel motor vessel, was unched in that year and is still operating on Windermere.

The *Swift* at Ambleside pier, 1908. The *Swift* entered service on Windermere in 1900. For a time she was the largest assenger steamer on the lake, built by T.B. Seath & Co. She remained in service until the 1990s when she was urned into a gallery to house the Campbell exhibition at Lakeside but is being scrapped at the time of writing.

The *Teal* (I) near Lakeside, 1909. Sister ship of the *Cygnet*, she was also built in 1879. A victim of the 192(recession, she was scrapped in 1927. The Furness Railway Company commissioned a series of photograph postcards of their steamer fleet from Raphael Tuck & Sons between 1909 and 1912. These, now collector items, were sold for 4*d* for a packet of six. The pictures on pp. 114–16 are from this series.

The steam yacht *Britannia*, 1908. The subtitle on the postcard states 'for hire by private parties o Windermere', although she was purchased as a director's yacht by the Furness Railway Company fror Colonel Ridehalgh of Fell Foot for £350 in 1907. She had cost the Colonel £12,000 when Sleath's c Rutherglen built her in 1879. The *Britannia* was in FR service from 1907 to 1915 only and was scrappe in 1919.

Broughton-in-Furness station, *c.* 1910. On p. 83 we saw Foxfield Junction where the Coniston branch left the Furness Railway main line. The first station on this branch was Broughton, where in this picture the 'steam motor train' awaits passengers for the Down line. The stationmaster was John Broadbent and a porter was Thomas Fox at the time the photograph was taken. The station was opened in 1859.

Woodland station, *c.* 1900. This postcard clearly shows the passing place afforded by Woodland station on this single branch line. The station included the post office which served the few surrounding farms. There seems little other reason for its existence.

Torver station, 24 March 1963. Preston Whiteley recorded the scene after the Coniston branch finally closed in 1962 (passenger services had finished in 1958). Torver station gave access to the small hamlet of farms and slaters' cottages. The road to Coniston was improved later by taking in a section of the railway track.

Coniston station, *c.* 1900. The 'steam motor train' is seen pulled in to the fine covered station designed by Paley of Lancaster. A line to the Coniston copper mines can be seen on the right. These, with the many slate quarries in the area, were the main reason for building the Coniston branch. The copper traffic was much reduced after the late nineteenth-century slump in copper prices.

Coniston, late nineteenth century. Two pictures of Coniston railway staff in the 1880s. The picture on the right is from a *carte de visite* by Shirtliff John Priest of Barrow-in-Furness showing James Pepper dressed in the Furness Railway uniform as junior clerk at the station. Below, he is seen again with other members of the staff with his back against an FR tank engine in the station. These pictures were taken at the start of a long and illustrious railway career. After experience in other railways he joined the Midland Railway offices at Derby from 1908, rising through the ranks until, in 1922, on the eve of the great amalgamations, he became Manager and Secretary of the Northern Counties Railway in Northern Ireland. The Northern Counties Railway became part of the LMS in 1923. James Pepper carried out many improvements in the railway until his retirement in 1931. During the 1880s and through into the early twentieth century James's family was famous in the Coniston/ Langdale area as being at the centre of the writer Ruskin's 'Langdale linen industry' and his mother taught King Edward VII's wife Alexandra in the 'gentle art' of lacemaking. His father was a quarryman and the family lived at Holme Ground, Tilberthwaite, a quarry manager's house which later became the property of Beatrix Potter, the famous children's writer, and is now owned by the National Trust. The Ruskin Museum at Coniston, the Armitt Library Museum at Ambleside and the Museum of Lakeland Life at Kendal include material about this remarkable family.

Coniston station, 1940s. An ex-LNWR Webb 2–4–2 No. 6683 is seen with a branch train at Coniston station. W.G. Collingwood quotes Arthur Severn in his *The Life and Work of John Ruskin*: 'The Professor dislikes railways very much . . . but Mr Ruskin's dislike of railways has been the text of a great deal of misrepresentation, and his use of them at all has been often quoted an inconsistency. As a matter of fact he has never objected to main lines of railway communication but he has strongly objected, in common with a vast number of people, to the introduction of railways into districts whose chief interest is in their scenery; especially where as in the English Lake District the scenery is in miniature easily spoiled by embankments and viaducts, and by rows of ugly buildings which usually grew up round a station and where the beauty of the landscape can only be felt in quiet walks or drives through it.' (Ruskin of course lived across the lake directly opposite Coniston station.) Pearson's 1900 *Gossipy Guide to the English Lakes* is very frank on the subject: 'Coniston is an ugly village in a situation of great natural beauty. The older houses, it is true, are picturesque – as where, indeed, in Lakeland are they not? – but the modern additions are obtrusive and commonplace, and the dismal railway station which overlooks everything, is appallingly conspicuous. Luckily the place is small. We wish we could add that the church or church yard constituted a redeeming feature . . . instead the locomotive shrieks just above and unromantic lodging houses stare immediately into it. Yet this is the burial place of John Ruskin!'

Gondola and *Lady of the Lake* at Coniston Pier, *c.* 1910. These steam yachts owned by the Furness Railway were pictured in Series No. 9 of Raphael Tuck's postcards (*see* p. 116). The *Gondola* was built in 1859 (for James Ramsden), and the *Lady of the Lake* in 1908. Together they provided a round-the-lake tour until the outbreak of the Second World War. While the *Lady of the Lake* was scrapped in 1950, the *Gondola* was left to rot at Nibthwaite until it was renovated for the National Trust by Vickers of Barrow between 1977 and 1980. Burrow's *Guide to the Lake District with practical hints for tourists* from the early 1920s says, 'While these steamer trips are very enjoyable, one has perforce to submit to a certain definite programme while taking them.' The fares are given as:

WATERHEAD TO LAKE BANK:

SINGLE		**RETURN**	
1ST CLASS	2ND CLASS	1ST CLASS	2ND CLASS
1*s* 0*d*	0*s* 9*d*	1s 8*d*	1*s* 2*d*
(Subject to 50% increase)		(Cycles on Coniston 9*d*)	

Author's note: For those interested in the Foxfield–Coniston branch of the Furness Railway, the Cumbrian Railways Association published a valuable record of its passing in 1985.

Branch line humour on an Edwardian postcard. It is unlikely that any passenger train using the branch could be termed an express as most were local stopper trains or, later, north-east to Blackpool holidaymakers' specials or the Durham miners' specials to Ulverston.

Ivatt 'Mogul' 2–6–0 No. 46470 at Tebay, 1950s. The engine is obviously doing a bit of shunting as the guard's van is next to the locomotive on the former North Eastern sidings at Tebay. This class was widely to be seen working Stainmore coke trains on the trains through Kirkby Stephen to the north-east in the later days of the line. A number of them were allocated to sheds in that area.

vatt 'Mogul' 2–6–0 No. 46475 at Tebay station heading the passenger train to Kirkby Stephen, 1952. This train possibly the nearest one could get to the 'Express' characterized in the picture on p. 122, although it must be id the engine front lamp shows express passenger duty. The stations on the line were at Gaisgill, avenstonedale and Smardale. The branch line from Tebay to Kirkby Stephen East station was part of an mazing joint venture by businessmen in the north-east, the Lancaster & Carlisle Railway and entrepreneurs in urness to bring Durham coke across to the rich ironworks of Furness, crossing Stainmore in the process *ee also* p. 128). The line opened in July 1861 for goods and August 1861 for passengers. It became part of the Iorth Eastern Railway (later London & North Eastern). Tebay and Clifton Moor (*see* p. 30) were the points vhere the North Eastern line met the LNWR but North Eastern shed and other facilities at Tebay were for nany years quite separate to the North Western. Services on the line were wound down over ten years from 952 to 1962. Passenger services went first in late 1952.

North Eastern Railway yard at Tebay, June 1963. The top photograph shows the use of the Tebay–Kirkby Stephen branch after closure. Then, at times, it seemed that the whole length was filled with parked trains of various sorts. Here we see a number of diesel railcars. Below, a double-headed train leaves Tebay for Kirkby Stephen and the north-east, a decade or so before closure. BR 2–6–0 No. 77003 obscures details of the second locomotive pulling the seven-carriage train, possibly a Blackpool train or Durham miners' special to and from Ulverston.

Closed Gaisgill station, 1962. This station was on what is now the route of the main A685 road, 2 miles from Tebay. The level-crossing and signal-box with signals have all disappeared but the station house remains. The station platform was removed in about 1952 when the passenger service ceased.

Ravenstonedale station, *c.* 1890. This lively scene was recorded by Yeoman of Barnard Castle. It shows a busy platform with staff and passengers waiting for the next local train. The station was actually at Newbiggin-on-Lune, about 2 miles away from Ravenstonedale village. The station building is now, as at Gaisgill, a private house.

Ravenstonedale station, March 1960. The railway line closed to passenger traffic in 1952 but it was still use for goods. On the reverse of this photograph is written, '2 BR 2–6–0s Nos 76050 and 76446 accept the toke through the now closed Ravenstonedale station, *en route* to Kirkby Stephen with empty hoppers, 19.3.60.'

Opposite: The viaduct at Smardale Gill, *c.* 1905. The 1905 Bulmer's *Guide* says of the parish of Waitby, 'Th North-Eastern and Midland Railways pass through the parish and are carried over the Scandale Beck, whic flows through the valley, upon two noble viaducts, of more than 100 ft in height. Smardale Stationmaste (N.E. Rly) Richard George Mallabar.' The North Eastern Railway viaduct is shown opposite. This now ha listed building status but was almost blown up in the 1970s by the Army who thought the operation woul make an interesting exercise! Before reaching Smardale station the NE line went under the majestic Midlan Railway viaduct (*see* p. 43).

Penrith station, *c.* 1920. North Eastern Railway engine 2–4–0 No. 1464 takes a passenger train from Penrith towards the Eden Valley line. The junction with the North Western main line was at Clifton where a station was built in 1927 (*see* p. 30).

Cliburn station, 1960s. The single track line with Cliburn signal-box and station buildings are seen here at about the time of the through-route closure in 1962. The route continued in use as a limestone quarry line to Merry Gill, Kirkby Stephen, until the 1970s and as a military line to Warcop until recently.

The photograph above shows Appleby East station complete with platform, *c.* 1962. The station still included a coal depot. The lower picture shows the same area in 1998. The railway track can still be seen although the platform has gone. A private group is currently trying to reopen the line to Warcop and has plans to develop further the Eden Valley line.

Near Warcop station, 1998. The railway line to Warcop still exists as it was used until recently by the Army to bring in material to the Warcop gun range. In the very few years of neglect since Army traffic ceased, nature has taken over.

Kirkby Stephen Junction, 1961. The delightful architecture of the North Eastern Railway stations extended to the signal-boxes. This example was built where the lines from Tebay and Penrith met north of Kirkby Stephen East station.

irkby Stephen East station yard, 1950s. Ex-North Eastern Railway J21 class 0–6–0 No. 65089 leaves Kirkby :ephen East station for Darlington in British Railways days. The train seems to have reverted to earlier railway :actice as it consists of a goods van and three passenger coaches. On the near side of the road bridge a busy ɔods station is seen, while on the further side the engine depot and passenger station is just visible. Little of iis scene can be traced today. Kirkby Stephen East station and the Midland station higher up the fell gave the wn two separate routes for many decades. Shopping in Carlisle was possible with both (change at Penrith on e NE). Visits to the Yorkshire towns were made via the Midland to Leeds. Journeys to the north-east towns ere possible on the NE via Barnard Castle and Darlington. A number of local businesses also used the railway bring in coal, oil and other goods and send out limestone, livestock and crates of dead rabbits. The North astern line also brought specials to Blackpool and the miners' convalescent home at Ulverston. The closure of e line put this traffic on to the roads with Kirkby Stephen becoming a 'service area' for the NE bus traffic. he two lines, in particular the depot attached to the North Eastern station, offered employment for many irkby Stephen men.

Merry Gill viaduct, Kirkby Stephen 1955. Ivatt 2–6–0 No. 46473 hauls a train of empty coke wagons over the viaduct at Hartley towards Stainmore. This line was opened as part of the route from the north-east to the Furness area iron and steel works. It closed when the industries declined.

Near Merry Gill, 1955. Heavy snowfall was always a major problem on the line over Stainmore. On 25 February 1955 an engine with snowplough had forced its way from Barnard Castle but became stuck in a snowdrift in the Hartley/Merry Gill area. Men were called to free it but they were unsuccessful for some time. Their efforts can be seen here, shown in discarded spadefuls of snow. Note the fence post, bottom right.

Belah viaduct. This remarkable lattice structure was opened to traffic in 1861 and the above photograph was taken soon afterwards. Forty years later it was reproduced as a postcard. The viaduct was also photographed by Preston Whiteley on 21 July 1963 as it was being demolished (below), following line closure. Hailed as a wonder of railway engineering in the nineteenth century, its demolition caused much controversy among railway enthusiasts. The viaduct was 1000 ft long, 200 ft high and was built in forty-three days in the summer of 1859. When the bridge was dismantled the following verse was found written on a paper tucked into it:

To future ages these lines will tell
Who built this structure o'er the dell
Gilkes Wilson with these eighty men
Raised Beelah's [sic] viaduct o'er the glen.

Belah signal-box, 1962. The remains of the railway after its closure in 1962 are clearly visible here. Part of the track had been lifted but the signal-box and line-side cabin appear to be intact.

Stainmore summit, 1950s. Wordsell class J21 0–6–0 No. 65033 is seen on the 1370 ft summit of Stainmore with a three-coach passenger train. Near here, further east, the line ran into County Durham via Barnard Castle.

Cockermouth, Keswick, and Penrith Railway

Cumberland Lakes & Mountains

LAKES.

Derwentwater, Buttermere,
Crummock, Ullswater,
Thirlmere, Bassenthwaite.

MOUNTAINS.

Skiddaw, Helvellyn, Scafell,
&c. &c.

GOLF LINKS.

Embleton, 18 holes. Keswick, 9 holes.

THIS RAILWAY affords the readiest access to the heart of the Lake District, and is in immediate connection with the London and North Western Main Line and North Eastern Railway at PENRITH. It also forms a connection with the London and North Western and Maryport and Carlisle Railways at Cockermouth, thus giving every facility for reaching the district from all parts.

Particulars of Arrangements and Bookings, see Company's Announcements.

Keswick Station. J. CLARK, Secretary & Manager.

Cockermouth, Keswick & Penrith Railway advertising from the E.J. Burrows' *Lake District Guide* just after the First World War.

Penrith, 5 August 1952. Ivatt 'Mogul' 2–6–0 engines Nos 46488 and (behind) 46448, neither more than a few years old at the time, stand at Penrith station on a summer's day. As can be seen on pp. 58 and 132, this class of locomotive served in many capacities on many of the ex-company lines in BR days. One of the trains seen above was for the NE line and the other for the CK&P.

Blencow station, July 1963. On the CK&P Preston Whiteley photographed the engine crew of an Ivatt 2–6–0 from the first passenger carriage window behind the engine as the train approached Blencow. This station was closed from 1952 to 1955 but reopened when DMUs were put in service. In 1968 all stations were reduced to unmanned halts and in 1972 passenger traffic ceased.

Blencow, 5 August 1947. In earlier days the Webb 'Cauliflower' 0–6–0 worked both goods and passenger traffic on the CK&P, and here LMS No. 8369 is at Blencow working a Workington to Penrith goods. Many of these ex-LNWR engines survived into LMS days and some, including this engine, into BR days but were withdrawn soon after nationalization.

Blencow, 1998. The line of the railway towards Penrith can be seen in this modern picture from the bridge over the road near the quarry at Blencow. The rails have gone and the CK&P is no more, although there have been suggestions that a line from Penrith to Keswick could be reopened. Many argued at the time of closure that a short-sighted action was being taken.

Flusco Lime Works, Blencow, 1950s. BR-built Ivatt 'Mogul' 2–6–0 No. 46426 collects a train of goods wagons from the lime works. This traffic kept the Penrith to Blencow section of the CK&P open for just a few months after the final closure of the rest of the line in 1972.

The Greta valley, 1940s. The climb from Keswick towards Troutbeck through the beautiful Greta/Glenderamackin valley is superbly caught here in a picture from the Neville Stead collection. The over forty-years-old ex-LNWR Webb 'Cauliflower' 0–6–0 No. 28484 hauls a passenger train towards Penrith from Keswick on a glorious summer's day. Some Webb 0–6–0s, such as this one, had had the figure 2 added in front of their number by the LMS during the 1940s.

Keswick station, 27 July 1963. DMUs were hailed as the saviours of the CK&P when they were introduced in 1955. Here the 6.55 p.m. to Penrith and the 6.42 p.m. to Workington wait side by side at Keswick. The through-line from Keswick and Cockermouth to Workington was closed in 1966 and the Penrith to Keswick route was shut down in 1972 when Keswick station was also closed.

Keswick station, 1950s. Ivatt 'Mogul' 2–6–0 No. 46449 with passenger train at Keswick. This engine was one of the class built by British Railways after it took over the LMS where the design originated. A number of examples of this popular engine were preserved when steam was abandoned in 1968.

Cockermouth station. Officially the end of the CK&P, Cockermouth station is seen above in about 1905. On the back of the postcard the Revd Mr Roscoe, Methodist Minister from Arnside, apologises to his son, saying that he was sorry he could not get an engine postcard. Below is a 1930s private photograph of the westbound platform. Note the steps on both platforms. Cockermouth station was closed in 1966. Between Keswick and Cockermouth were Braithwaite, Bassenthwaite Lake and Embleton stations. Pictures of these by Preston Whiteley can be found in *Keswick and the Central Lakes in Old Photographs* by John Marsh (Sutton, 1993).

West from Cockermouth. Between Cockermouth and Workington was the London & North Western line via Brigham Junction (with the Maryport & Carlisle Railway), Broughton Cross, Marron Junction (with the Whitehaven, Cleator & Egremont Railway), Camerton and Workington Bridge. A number of these stations were closed before the Second World War. The picture above shows the proud staff at Brigham Junction (*see also* p. 92) well before the final closures of 1964–66, and below is the dismal scene on 16 April 1966 at Camerton station, which had been closed in 1952.

The Waverley Line, 1960. The North British Railway brought its Waverley Line into Carlisle from Edinburgh in 1862. In 1924 North British became part of the London & North Eastern Railway. The route was closed in 1969/70. Only a small part of the Waverley was in Cumbria – from the border with Scotland at Kershope Foot through Longtown into Carlisle. Above is 'Britannia' 4–6–2 No. 70044 *Earl Haig* with the Up 'Waverley Express' on 27 August 1960 at Carlisle. Below is ex-LNER D49 4–4–0 No. 62744 *The Holderness* (named after a hunt of that name) passing the signal-box and level-crossing at Longtown on 29 July 1960.

Longtown, 29 July 1960. Another ex-LNER monster is seen at Longtown. In this picture 1930s Gresley V2 class 2–6–2 No. 60816 roars by with a mixed goods train. *Green Arrow*, the first in this class, was preserved as steam was withdrawn with its original LNER number 4771. The Waverley Line was an amazing line for train-spotters as one never knew what would turn up next.

Scotch Dyke at Kirkandrews on Esk, 1998. A forlorn picture of ex-railway days can be found where the Waverley Line neared the Scottish border. The station platform buildings and houses can still be seen but there are no rails where those wonderful steam engines used to run. Near here, at Riddings Junction, the line divided with a branch to Langholm and a few miles further on the main line left Cumbria at Kershope Foot (*see also* p. 2).

Alston, 29 July 1952. This double-headed passenger train from Haltwistle, pictured pulling into Alston station, was part of the LNER's operation in the north Pennines. In the background is the once busy goods yard. Even though this picture was taken in British Railways days little had changed on the branch since private ownership. Gresley J39 0–6–0 No. 64816 heads a nineteenth-century Worsdell G5 0–4–4 tank engine No. 67315. Alston was also connected – via Brampton Junction on the Newcastle to Carlisle line – to Carlisle. Only a very few miles of this Pennine branch were in Cumbria and it is often omitted from books on Cumbrian railways because it belonged so much to the north-east. Opened in 1852, the branch closed in 1976. The South Tynedale Railway Preservation Society has opened a narrow gauge railway on part of the old trackbed from Alston and hopes to extend this as funds became available. The old signal-box on the left of the picture has been replaced on the narrow gauge railway by another (*see* p. 145). The station buildings are now home to the very helpful Alston Tourist Information Office and a café.

Alston, 1998. The modern scene at Alston station is so different from that in branch line days. Car parks occupy land once covered by rail. This picture is an interesting 'now' comparison to the 'then' on p. 144. The narrow gauge railway started running in 1984 with constant expansion as its aim.

The Alston branch, 1 January 1962. Harsh winters often blocked the roads but not the rails to Alston and the branch closure was delayed because of this consideration. Here the Alston branch snow plough is at work at Slaggyford, about 5 miles into Northumberland from Alston. Ex-North British and LNER class J36 0–6–0 No. 65237 from Carlisle Canal shed pushes a snow plough originally from the Kirkby Stephen depot which closed in 1962.

'Our local express to Silloth' was more branch line humour from Cynicus (above). The picture is the same as those seen on pp. 18 and 101 on other branches but the wording was altered to suit the particular outlet. Below, a North British Railway 4–4–0 No. 36 is seen leaving Carlisle possibly in the late nineteenth-century on a Silloth express not too unlike the Cynicus train. The North British Railway brought the Waverley Line to Carlisle in 1862 and became part of the LNER in 1924. The line to Silloth was opened in 1856 by a local company, but within ten years the North British Railway had taken it over as it wanted to acquire access to the port for its increasing business. Silloth was growing as a resort also and for many years the branch brought eager seaside holidaymakers to the Solway coast.

Drumburgh to Port Carlisle. The spur of line to Port Carlisle from the Carlisle to Silloth railway ran from Drumburgh station to Glasson and then on to Port Carlisle using the filled in canal as its route. This was the original conversion of the Carlisle Canal into a railway in 1854. In 1856 the Silloth Bay railway was built from Drumburgh to Silloth leaving Port Carlisle as a branch because Silloth was developed as the new docks for Carlisle. From 1857 the branch used a horse for drawing a passenger 'Dandy' along the rails and goods were moved, when required, by steam locomotives. The picture above shows the horse 'Dandy' with its back to Carlisle at Port Carlisle station. This amazing horse-drawn system survived until 1914 when, after track repairs, it was replaced by steam locomotion. The last 'Dandy' coach survived as a curiosity and can now be seen in the National Railway Museum at York. The photograph below was taken by Carlisle photographer Tassell to show the first North British Railways steam-hauled passenger train at Port Carlisle station on 6 April 1914. The NBR 0–6–0 tank No. 22's fireman was William Matthews (centre) whose son, John, has kindly allowed this 84-year-old family picture to be included in this book.

The Solway viaduct. To avoid the detour through Carlisle, the Solway Junction Railway built the viaduct over the estuary of the Solway from near Bowness-on-Solway in Cumbria to near Annan on the Scottish side. The iron ore from Cumberland could thus be transported to the Lanarkshire ironworks at lower cost. The viaduct was opened in September 1869 for goods and for passengers the following July. By 1895 the Caledonian Railway had taken over the line although it was reported to have run the route for the Solway Junction Company since inception. For a brief period this spectacular crossing carried both goods and passengers, but then the iron ore traffic declined and during the First World War passenger traffic was withdrawn. All traffic ceased in 1921 owing, it was said, to the unsafe condition of the viaduct but repairs were never carried out and the bridge was dismantled in 1933. Below, the huge embankment on the Cumbrian side is a landmark even today.

Silloth. This photograph shows the full extent of the railway yard at Silloth with the docks on the left and the mill and station on the right. The station finally closed with nasty scenes – nearly 10,000 people demonstrated in September 1964 as the old North British Railway route between Carlisle and its port was severed. It was to Silloth station that thousands of Carlisle holidaymakers came on their way to the seaside by both scheduled and special trains, and the removal of the facility caused much anger.

Silloth, 1999. The desolate scene today at Silloth station. The platform that carried so many holidaymakers and the station buildings are still to be seen but only as overgrown and bricked-up relics.

Moor Row, 1950s. Ex-LMS Fowler 4F 0–6–0 No. 44549 – shed No. 12A for Carlisle Kingmoor – stands wit a mixed train of coaches at Moor Row station. This stop was the first on the climb from Whitehaven after th Mirehouse Junction and was opened in 1857. Closure was a long process from the 1930s onwards. Passenge services at Moor Row should have ceased in 1947 but workmen's specials and excursion trains continued t call at this once very busy station with its sidings. The station deteriorated through the 1950s but a line fror Mirehouse through to the Beckermet iron ore mines continued into the 1980s. Bulmer's 1901 *Directory* *Cumberland* says: 'The introduction of the "iron way" has completely revolutionised the financial an commercial relations of the district through which they pass. . . . To extend and expedite the stream c communication is to accelerate the current of commerce, to give an impulse to the flood of prosperity, and fructifying and beneficial circulation of a floating capital. Railways call into action a vast quantum of manu labour and unappropriated wealth, and by finding employment for the surplus population, greatly increase th prosperity of the Nation. They have a beneficial effect on manufactures, mines, . . . and they may be said t form the most important item in the development of the mineral wealth of the district. THE WHITEHAVE CLEATOR & EGREMONT COMPANY was incorporated by act of Parliament in 1854. The line was originall only seven miles in length but, by extension of powers, it has been carried on to Workington. This branc opened for passenger traffic on 1 October 1879, has an entire length of 21½ miles.'

Moor Row, October 1966. Even as late as 1966 it was possible to think that Moor Row was still important. The extensive sidings, the platforms and the signal-box were still intact but close examination reveals there were missing railings and broken walls by this time.

Woodend station, October 1966. The level-crossing at Woodend and the station were still intact and in fact all looked neat and tidy. The station was opened in 1880 about half-way between Moor Row and Egremont and closures of services over a number of decades left the line here as the last of the Whitehaven, Cleator & Egremont Railway stations to be closed to goods traffic; it survived until Beckermet iron ore mine closed in 1980.

Beckermet station, *c.* 1910. Beckermet was the first station on the lines from Sellafield through Egremont to Moor Row and is here seen with staff posed on the platform. The line finally closed for goods in 1980 as the nearby iron ore mine finished production.

Yeathouse, *c.* 1900. One of the smaller stations on the WC&E lines was at Yeathouse between Rowrah and Frizington. It replaced nearby Eskett in 1875 when subsidence caused difficulty on that line of track and a new route was built.

Winder station, October 1966. Between Yeathouse (*see* p. 152) and Rowrah (below) was Winder. The goods line then in operation can be seen but this was to close in 1967. The passenger station had been closed during the 1930s Depression and had become a private house.

Rowrah station, October 1966. In the maze of lines to Rowrah Quarry and Kelton mines (Cleator & Workington Railway) was Rowrah station on the WC&E line to Marron Junction from Moor Row. The line lost its passenger traffic in 1931 and its well-built station houses became private dwellings. Although the platform can be seen here the line is well away from it. A coal depot in the station yard survived for many years.

Lamplugh station, October 1966. When the station was opened in 1866 the name Wright Green was used but this was changed in 1901. The great Depression saw the closure of the line from Moor Row up to Marron. Thirty-five years after closure the scene was bleak indeed.

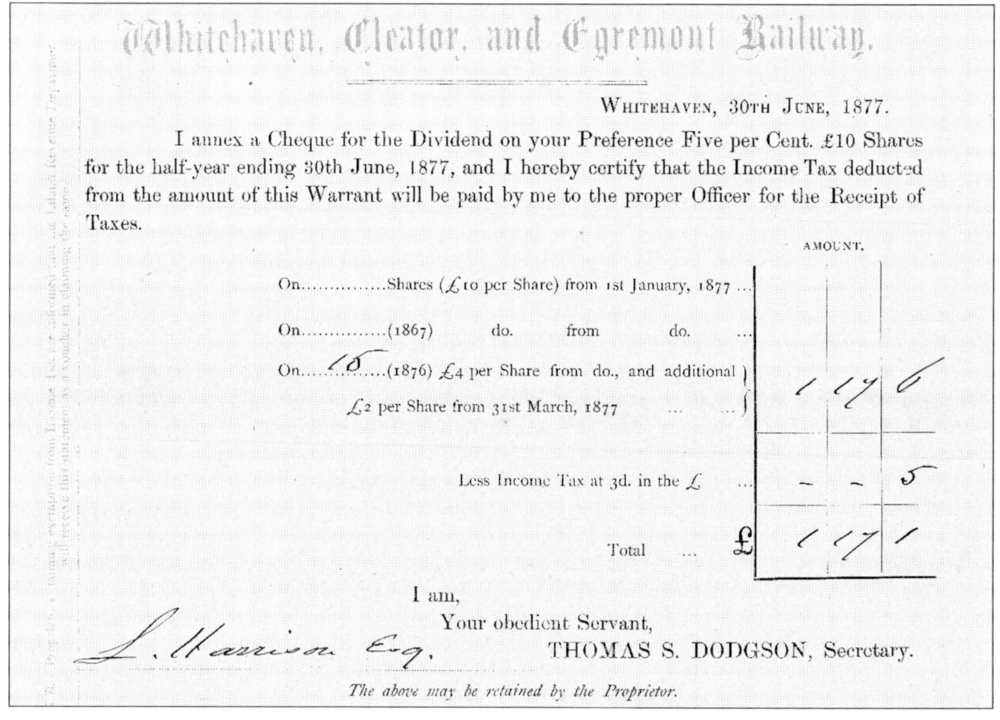

Whitehaven, Cleator, and Egremont Railway.

WHITEHAVEN, 30TH JUNE, 1877.

I annex a Cheque for the Dividend on your Preference Five per Cent. £10 Shares for the half-year ending 30th June, 1877, and I hereby certify that the Income Tax deducted from the amount of this Warrant will be paid by me to the proper Officer for the Receipt of Taxes.

	AMOUNT.		
On..............Shares (£10 per Share) from 1st January, 1877 ...			
On..............(1867) do. from do. ...			
On.....15.....(1876) £4 per Share from do., and additional £2 per Share from 31st March, 1877	1	17	6
Less Income Tax at 3d. in the £ ...	–	–	5
Total ... £	1	17	1

I am,
Your obedient Servant,
THOMAS S. DODGSON, Secretary.

L. Harrison Esq.

The above may be retained by the Proprietor.

Share dividend certificate, 1877. This dividend certificate showing the payment for the half year to June 1877 on fifteen 1876 £4 preference shares comes from the time of expansion and growth in the WC&E Railway. This was also the time of amalgamations as the Furness and London & North Western Railways started to take more than an interest through the joint committee system where the individual companies found ways of mutual working through a committee of senior staff from each firm.

Distington station, late nineteenth century. This is an interesting picture of two saddle tank locomotives from different companies in Distington station. The engine crew and station staff pose for the photographer. These are saddle tank locomotives Cleator & Workington Junction Railway No. 5 and Whitehaven, Cleator & Egremont Railway No. 111. These small West Cumberland railway companies' lines met at Distington station.

Cleator Moor station, October 1966. The closures of the iron ore mines and ironworks in West Cumberland brought about the end of several railway lines over many years. Final closure came to Cleator Moor in 1963 with trees and grass quickly taking over the once tidy scene. This station was originally on the Whitehaven, Cleator & Egremont Railway, where there was a junction with the Cleator & Workington Junction Railway (*see also* p. 159).

The Cleator & Workington Junction Railway.

Weighing Machine Ticket No. 276

Arlecdon Station, Dec 7 1920

Whose Cart Mr Charlton

Carter Do.

GOODS.	GROSS.			TARE.			NETT.		
	T.	C.	Q.	T.	C.	Q.	T.	C.	Q.
Meadow Hay		14	2		6	3		6	3
					7	2		7	0

J Ray *Weigher.*

Special Debit Book Folio............

Arlecdon station. This 1920 weighing machine ticket shows one of the facilities that a local station such as Arlecdon offered its surrounding population. On 7 December 1920 Mr Charlton with his own cart called at the station and had weighed seven hundredweights of meadow hay. (The amended arithmetic with the extra hundredweight is interesting.) The picture below shows how the station looked on 2 October 1966 when Preston Whiteley called at Arlecdon during his survey of closed lines. Arlecdon was shut down in the 1930s.

Workington shed, 1927. Ex-Cleator & Workington 0–6–0 saddle tank locomotive No. 8 *Hutton Hall* with its LMS No. 11566. Most of the five engines of this class taken over by the LMS were scrapped in the 1920s or 1930s but one survived until 1956. Bulmer's *Guide to Cumberland* of 1901 tries to explain the position with regard to the railway stations at Workington, for here the London & North Western and the Cleator & Workington Junction railways vied for business and the use of the docks. The Furness and Maryport & Carlisle Railways also had an interest, running over lines of other companies: 'The station of the Workington and Cleator Railway is in John Street and was built when the railway opened in 1879. It is a neat convenient station, quite adequate to suit its present requirements. The London & North Western Railway Company have their principal station at the low end of the town – hence it has always been locally known as the Low station. In 1881 a commodious goods yard and buildings were erected and in 1886 the company followed this up by entirely rebuilding the passenger station. At the same time the old-fashioned level-crossing was abolished, a substantial viaduct being substituted to give access to the harbour and marsh side. Workington Bridge station was also rebuilt in 1881.'

Workington sheds, April 1963. Ivatt 'Mogul' 2–6–0 No. 46488 (*see also* p. 136).

Seaton station, 16 April 1966. On the Linefoot to Calva Junction section of the Cleator & Workington Junction Railway was Seaton station, closed in the 1920s. The single line seen in this photograph was used to access the naval supply base at Buck Hill.

Great Broughton station, 1966. This desolate sight shows the remains of the buildings at Great Broughton station. It was closed during the cut-backs of the 1920s and '30s on the Seaton to Linefoot branch of the Cleator & Workington Junction Railway. The colliery traffic ceased in the 1930s but a line from Workington was left to serve Broughton Moor naval ammunition supply depot.

Even more desolation at Cleator Moor West station, October 1966. The station was shut down in the Depression years of the 1930s and the line here was finally closed in 1963.

Branthwaite station, October 1966. This rural view by Preston Whiteley in his survey of the closed West Cumberland railways shows the site of Branthwaite station on the Whitehaven, Cleator & Egremont Railway. Dating from 1866, the line from Marron Junction to Cleator Moor ceased carrying passengers in 1931 and was closed to goods in 1954.

Index

Aisgill 39, 40, 41
Alston 144, 145
Ambleside 115
Appleby East 129
Appleby West 45
Arlecdon 156
Armathwaite 48
Arnside 61, 62, 101
Askam-in-Furness 82

Barbon 99
Barrow-in-Furness 73–81, 96
Beckermet 152
Beckfoot 86
Belah 133, 134
Blencow 136, 137
Blea Moor 38
Boot 86
Bowness-on-Windermere 114
Brampton 52
Branthwaite 159
Brigham 92, 141
Broughton-in-Furness 117
Burneside 16
Burton & Holme 10

Camerton 141
Cark 66, 67
Carlisle 4, 9, 32–5, 48–51, 54–7, 91, 94–6, 142, 146
Cleator Moor East 155
Cleator Moor West 159
Cliburn 128
Clifton Moor 30
Cockermouth 140
Coniston 118–21
Cotehill 47
Crosby Garrett 43, 44

Dalton in Furness 72
Dallam Bridge 104, 105
Dent 37, 38
Dillicar 24
Distington 155

Eskmeals 84

Flusco 138
Foxfield 83

Gaisgill 125
Grange-over-Sands 59, 63–5, 101
Grayrigg 22, 23
Great Broughton 92, 158
Greenodd 108, 109

Harrington 89
Haverthwaite 110
Heversham 106
Hincaster 107

Kendal 16, 101
Kents Bank 66
Keswick 138, 139
Kingmoor 36, 49, 54, 57
Kirkandrews on Esk 143
Kirkby-in-Furness 82
Kirkby Lonsdale 98
Kirkby Stephen East 122, 130, 131
Kirkby Stephen West 37, 42

Lakeside 112–14, 116
Lamplugh 154
Lindal in Furness 71
Longmarton 45
Longtown 142, 143
Lowgill 100

Mallerstang 42
Maryport 93, 94, 95
Merrygill 132
Middleton in Lunesdale 99
Millom 84
Milnthorpe 11
Moor Row 150, 151

Newby Bridge 111

Oxenholme 12–15, 22

Patterdale 46
Penrith 31, 58, 128, 135, 136
Port Carlisle 147

Ravenglass 85, 86
Ravenstonedale 125, 126
Rowrah 153

Sandside 102, 103, 104
Seaton 158
Scout Green 27
Sedbergh 97, 100
Shap 28, 29
Siddick 90
Silloth 146, 149
Solway Viaduct 148
Smardale 43, 127
Stainmore 134
Staveley 17

Tebay 6, 24–6, 53, 122–4
Torver 118

Ulverston 68–70, 108

Warcop 130
Wetheral 53
Whitehaven 88, 89
Winder 153
Windermere 3, 18–21
Woodend 151
Woodland 117
Workington 87, 90, 157

Yeathouse 152